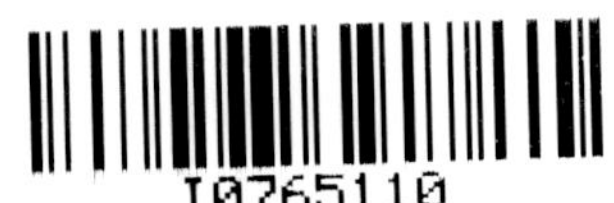

coloring book fun with beautiful butterflies Designs

THIS BOOK BELONGS TO

Date:

Color test page

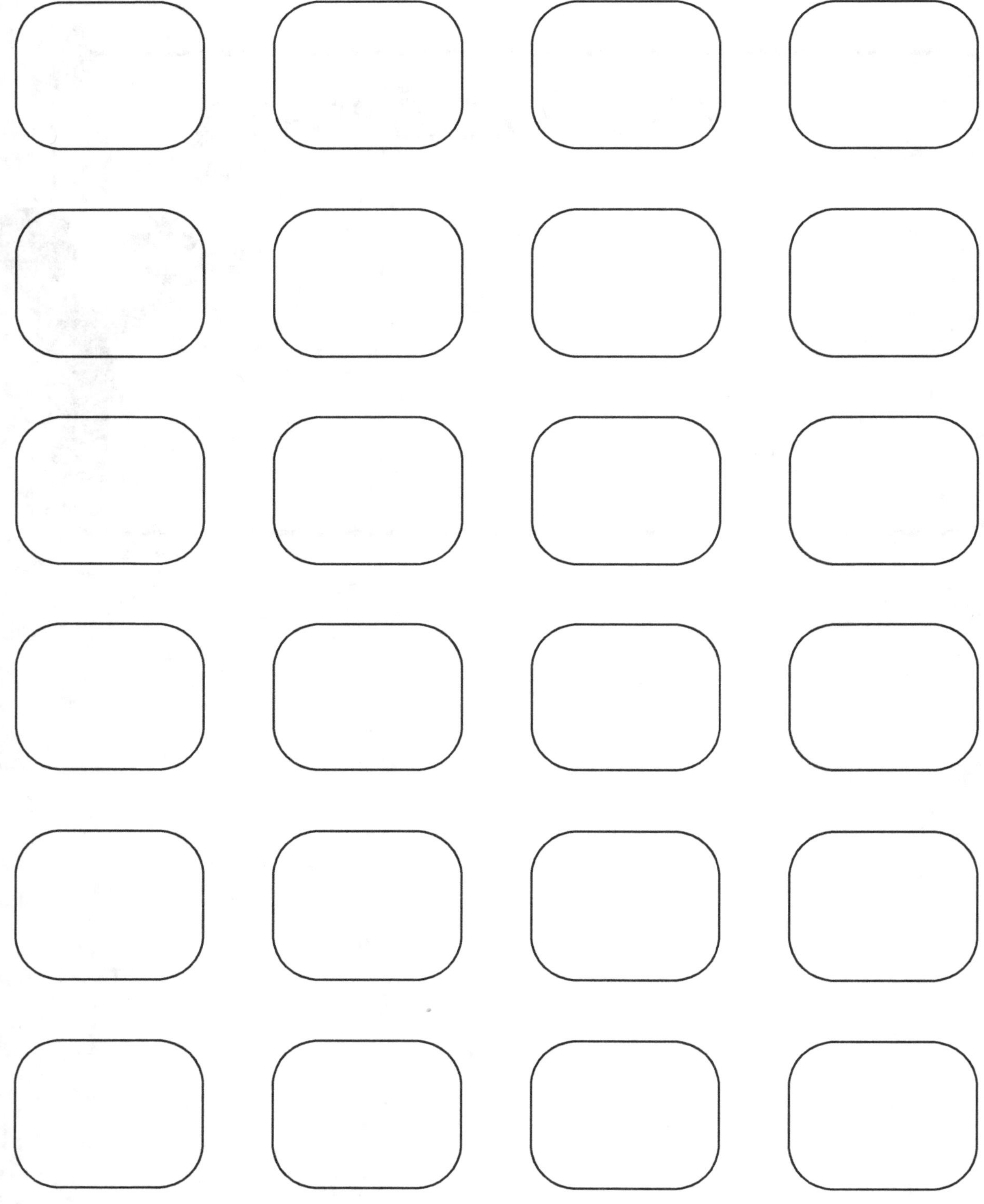

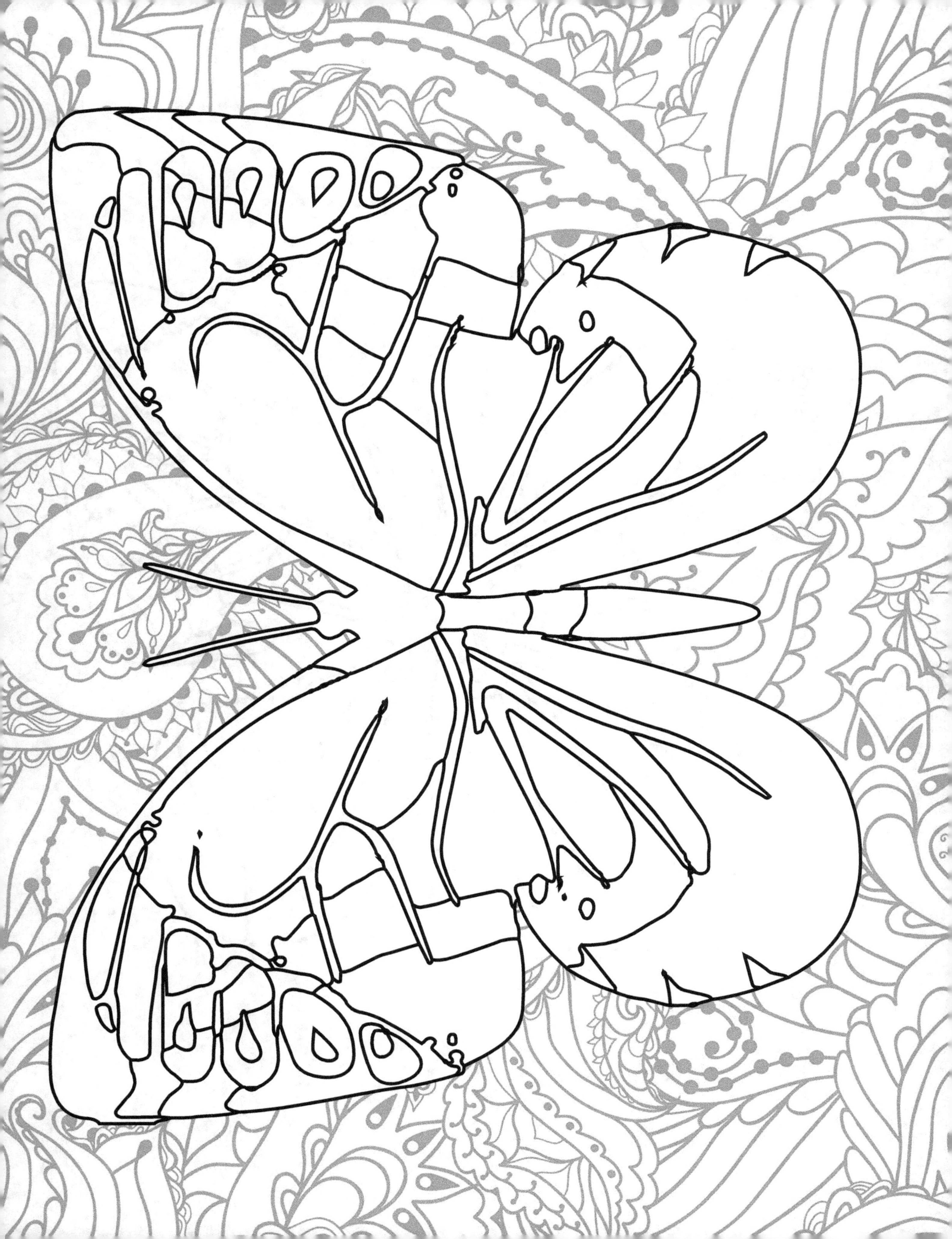

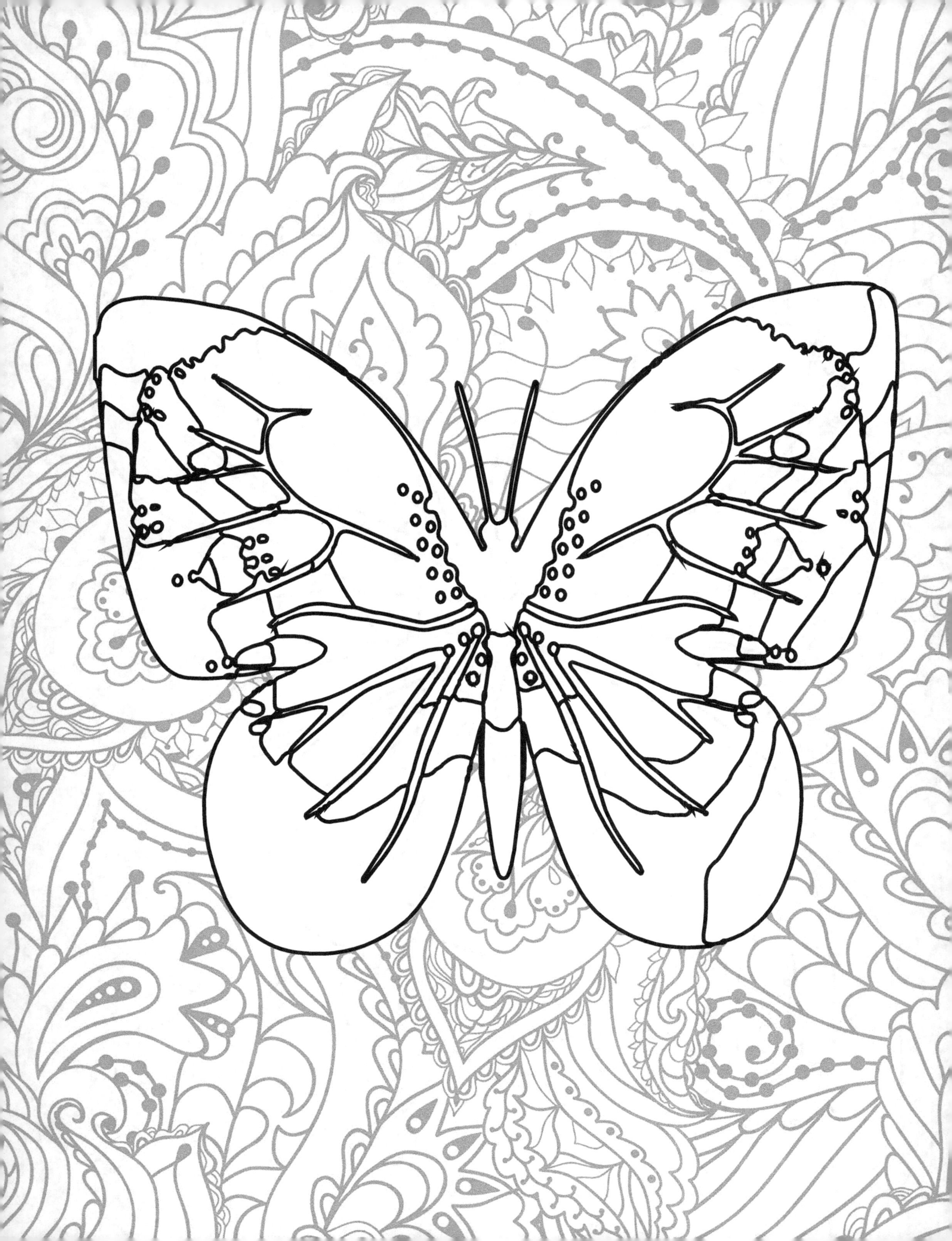

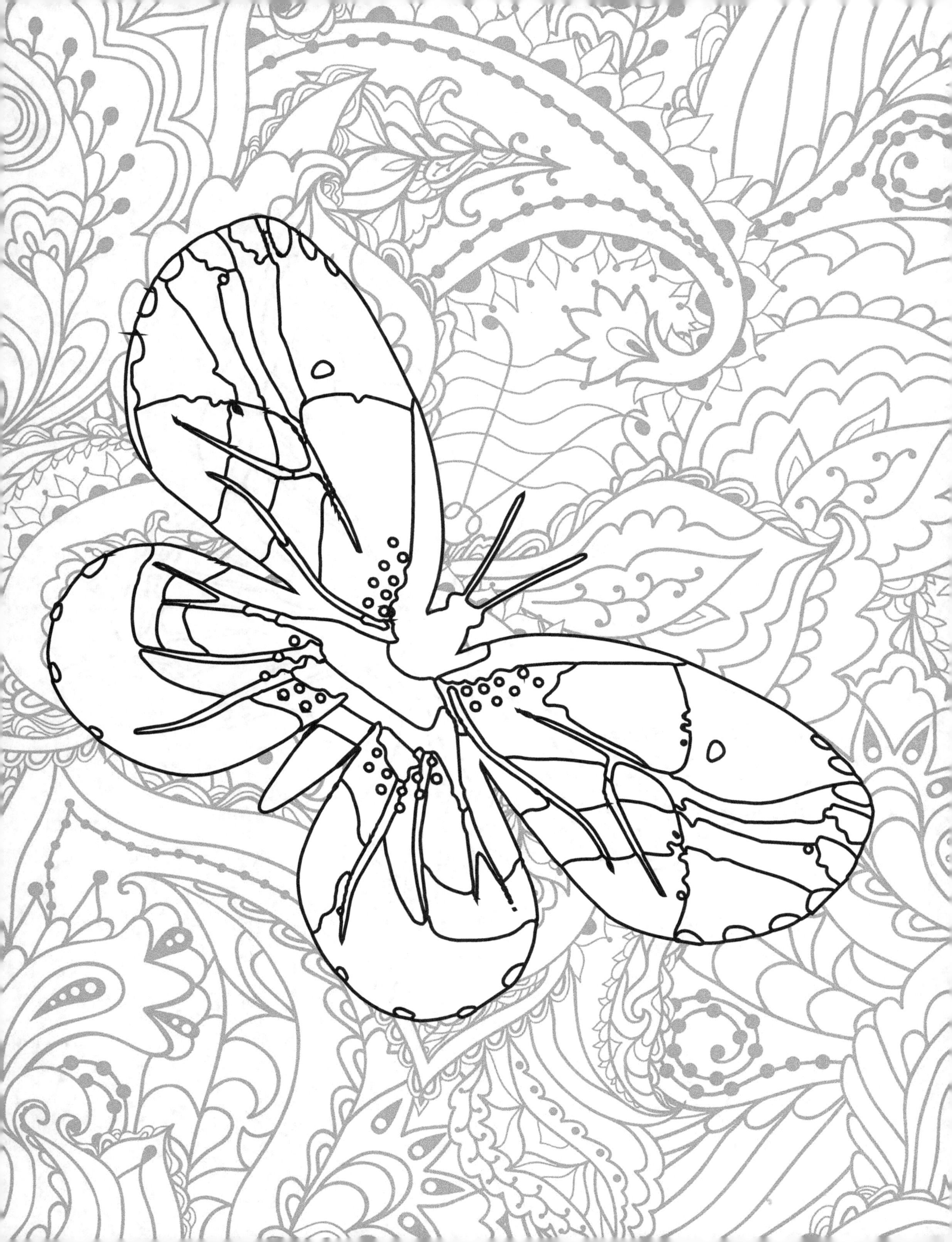

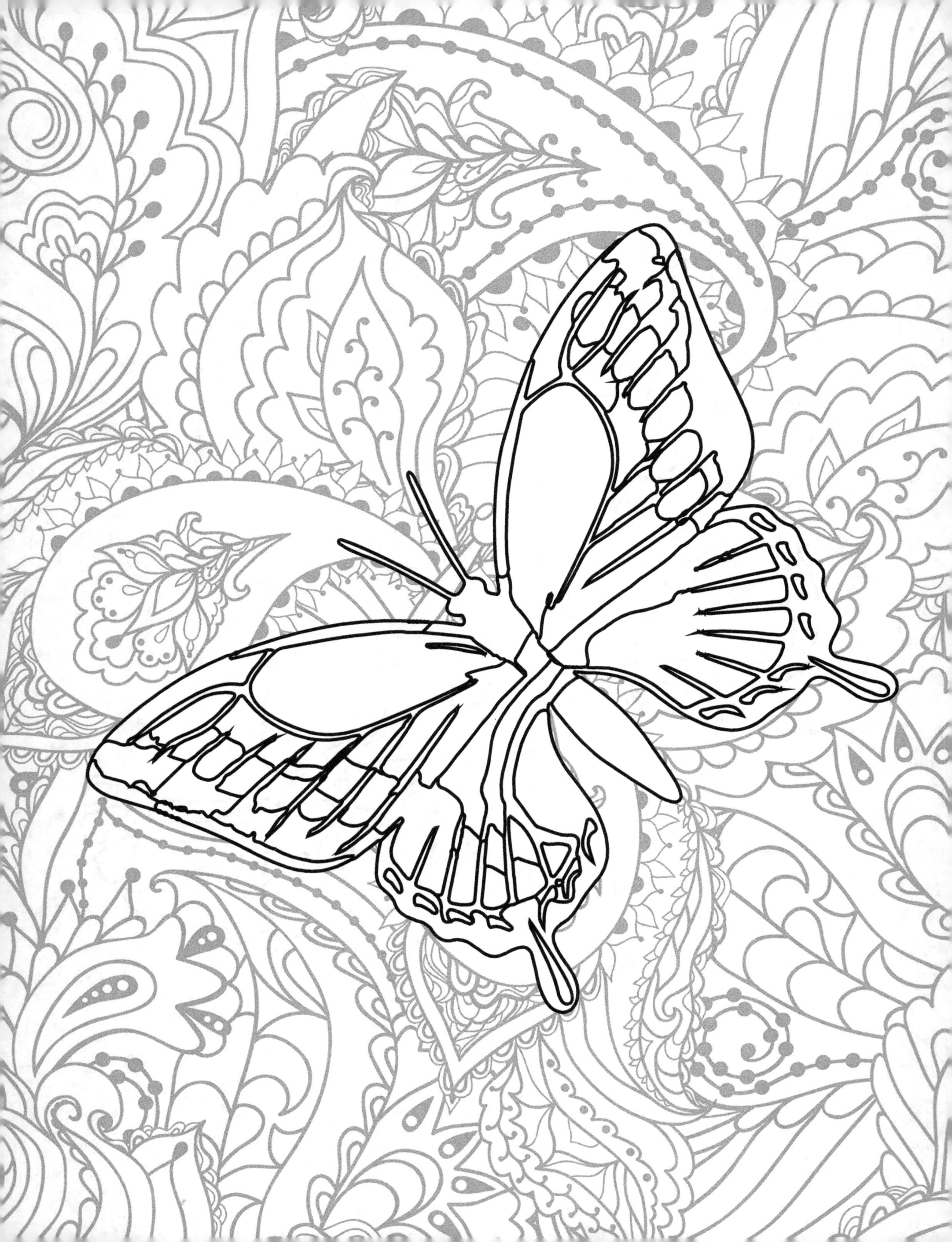

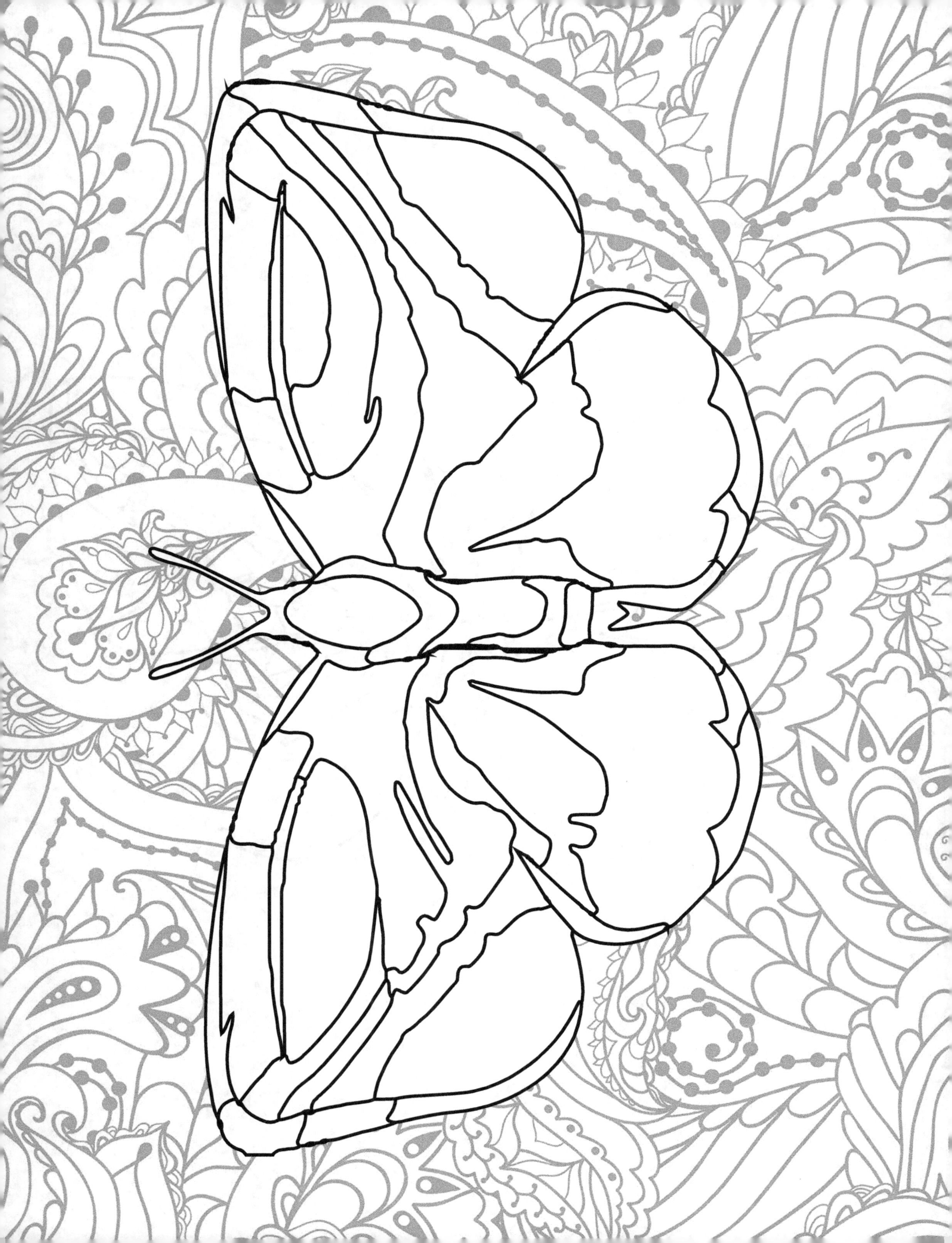

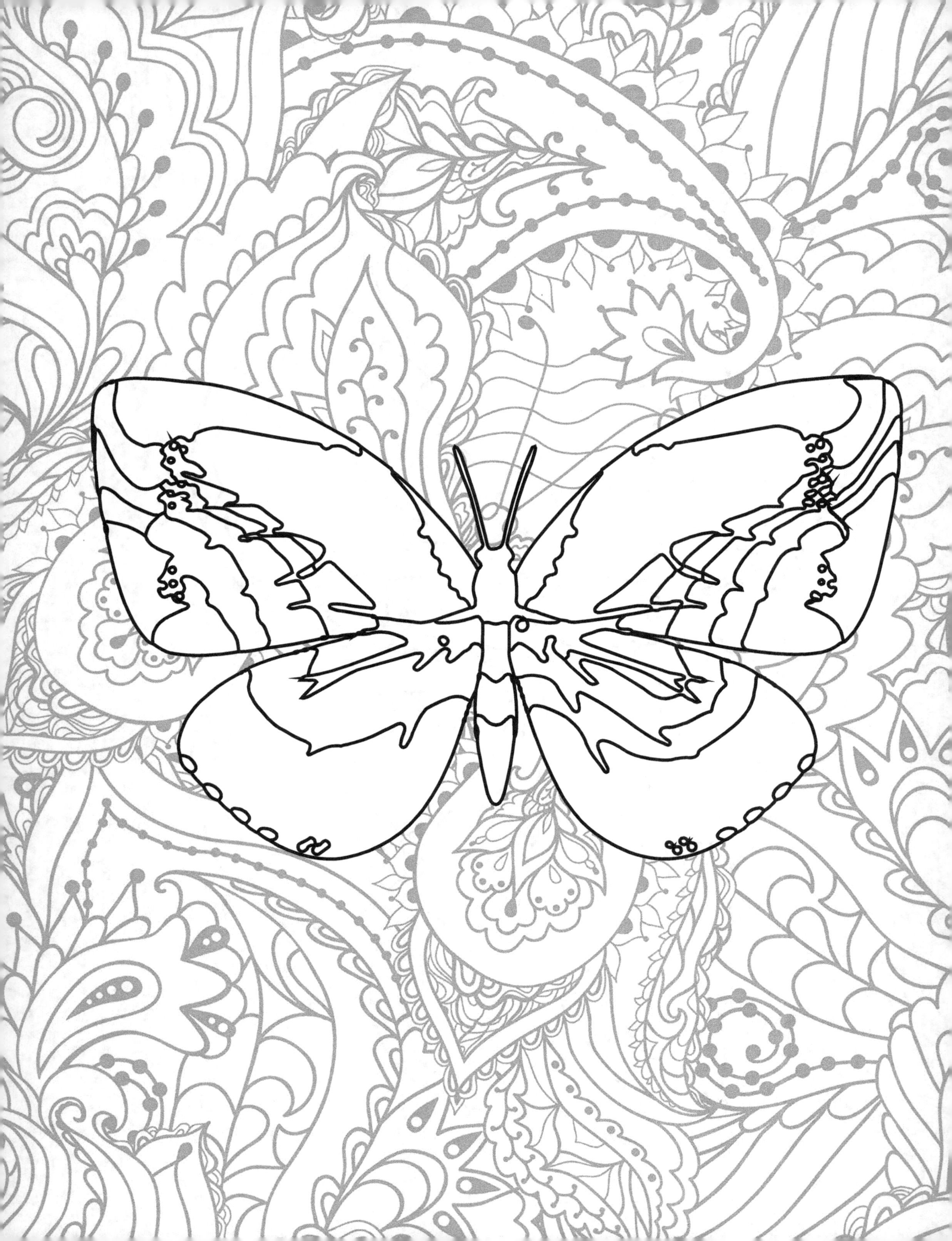

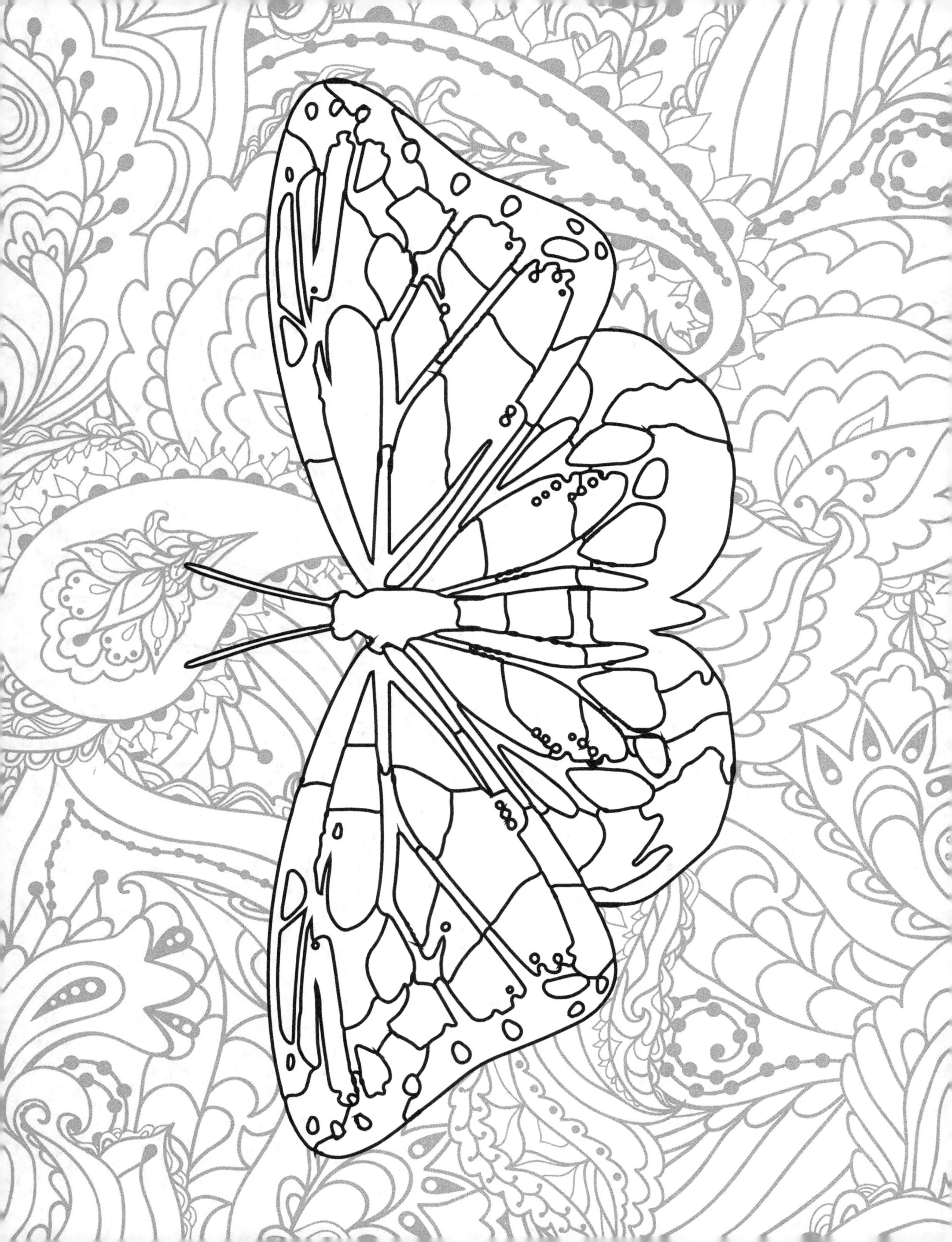

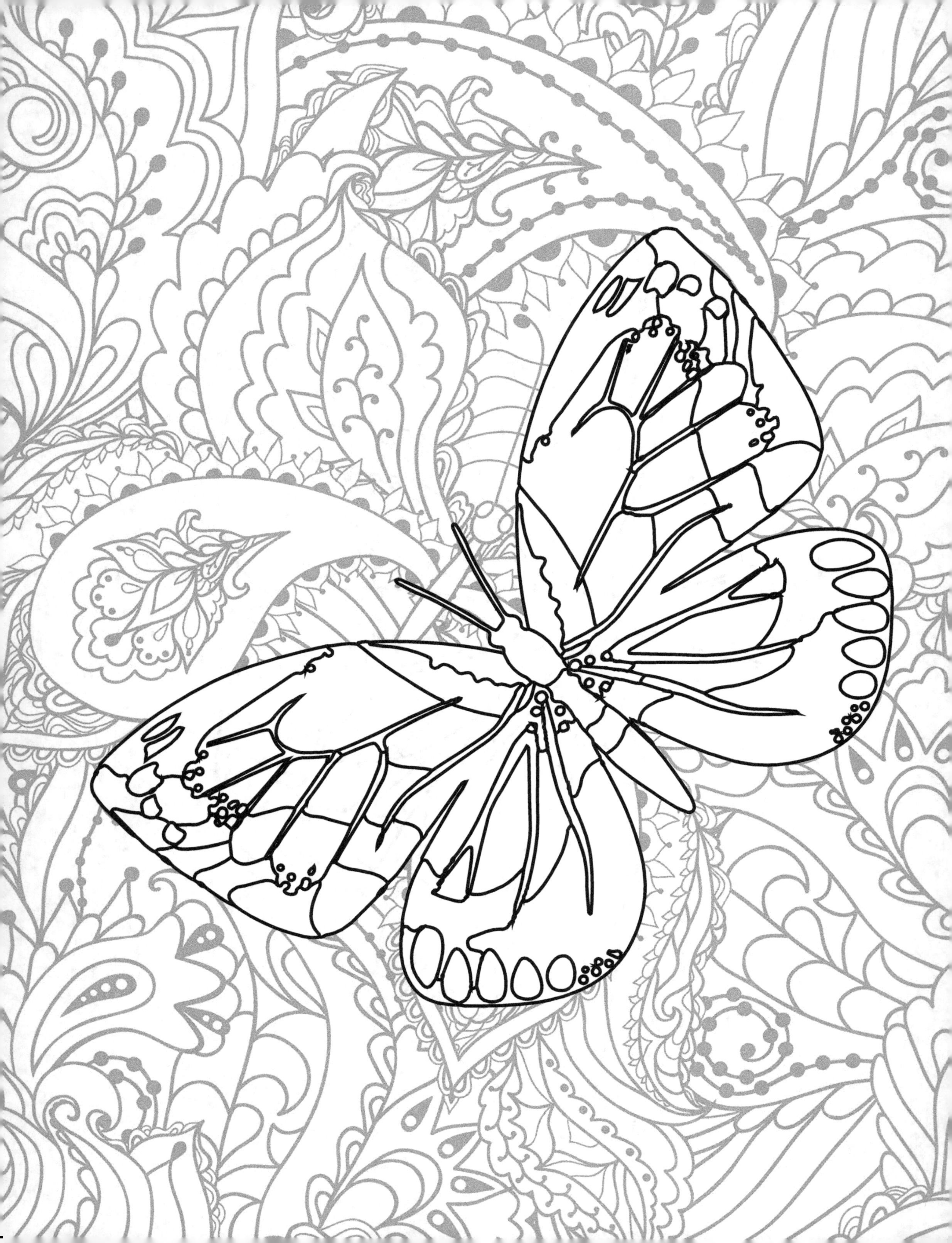

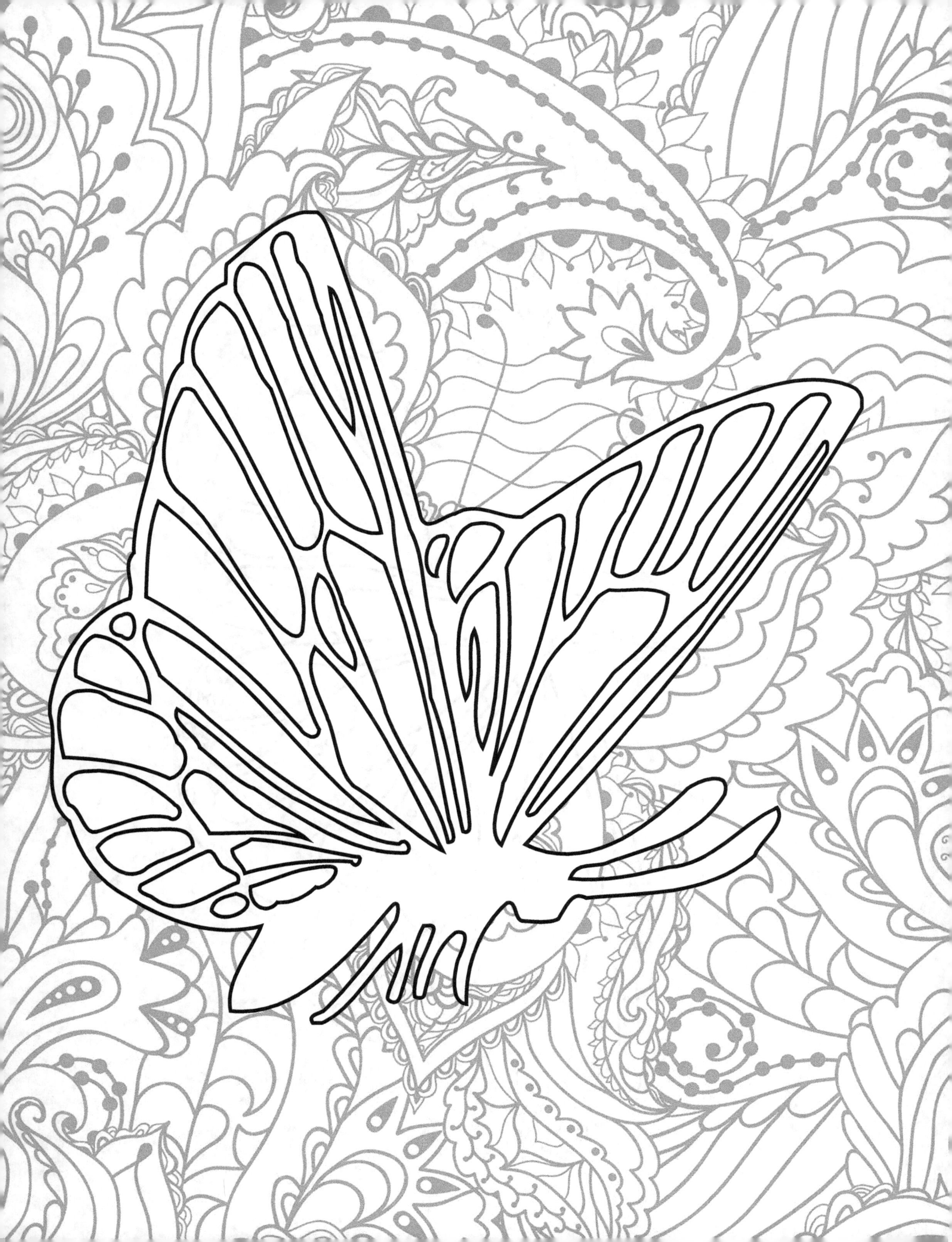

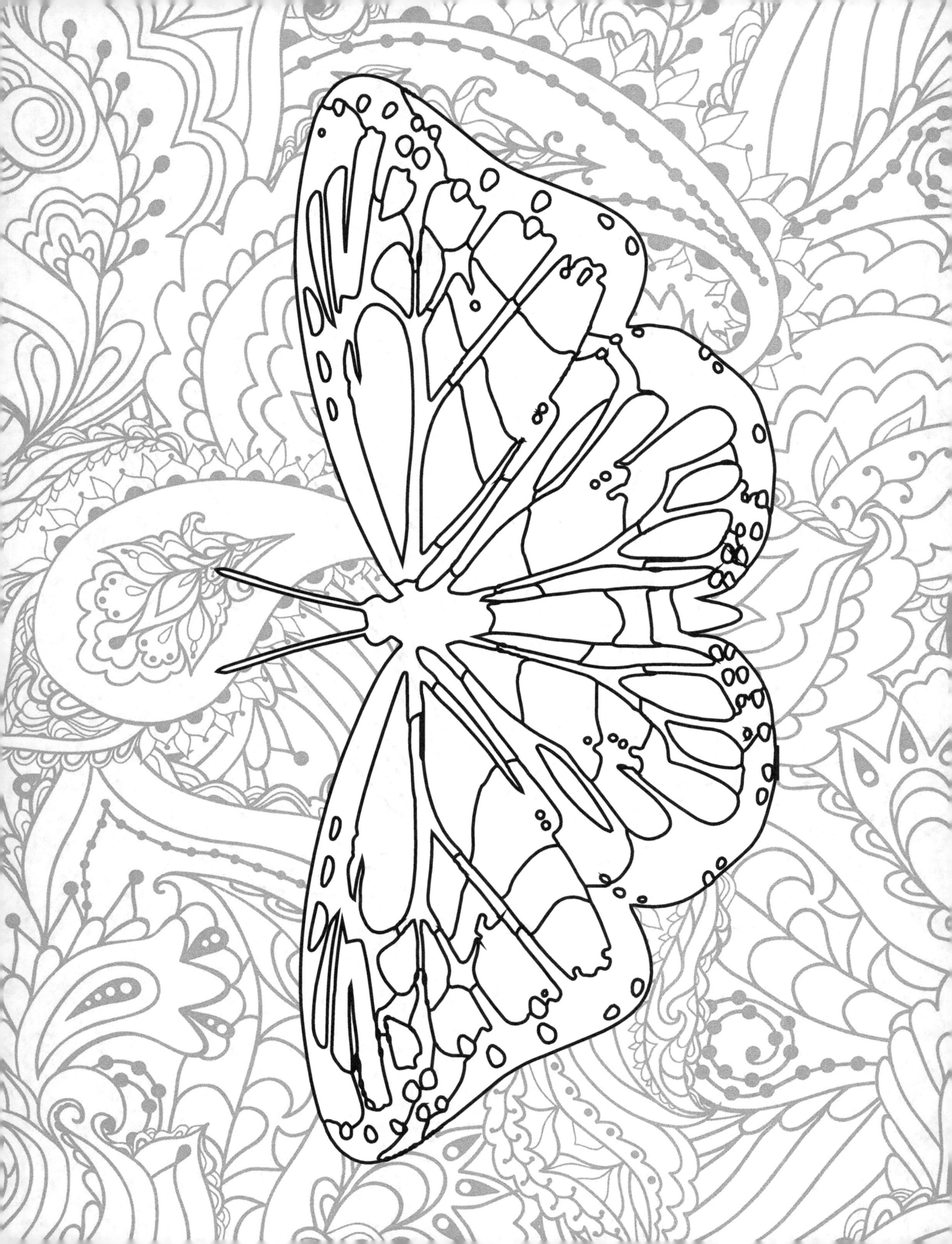

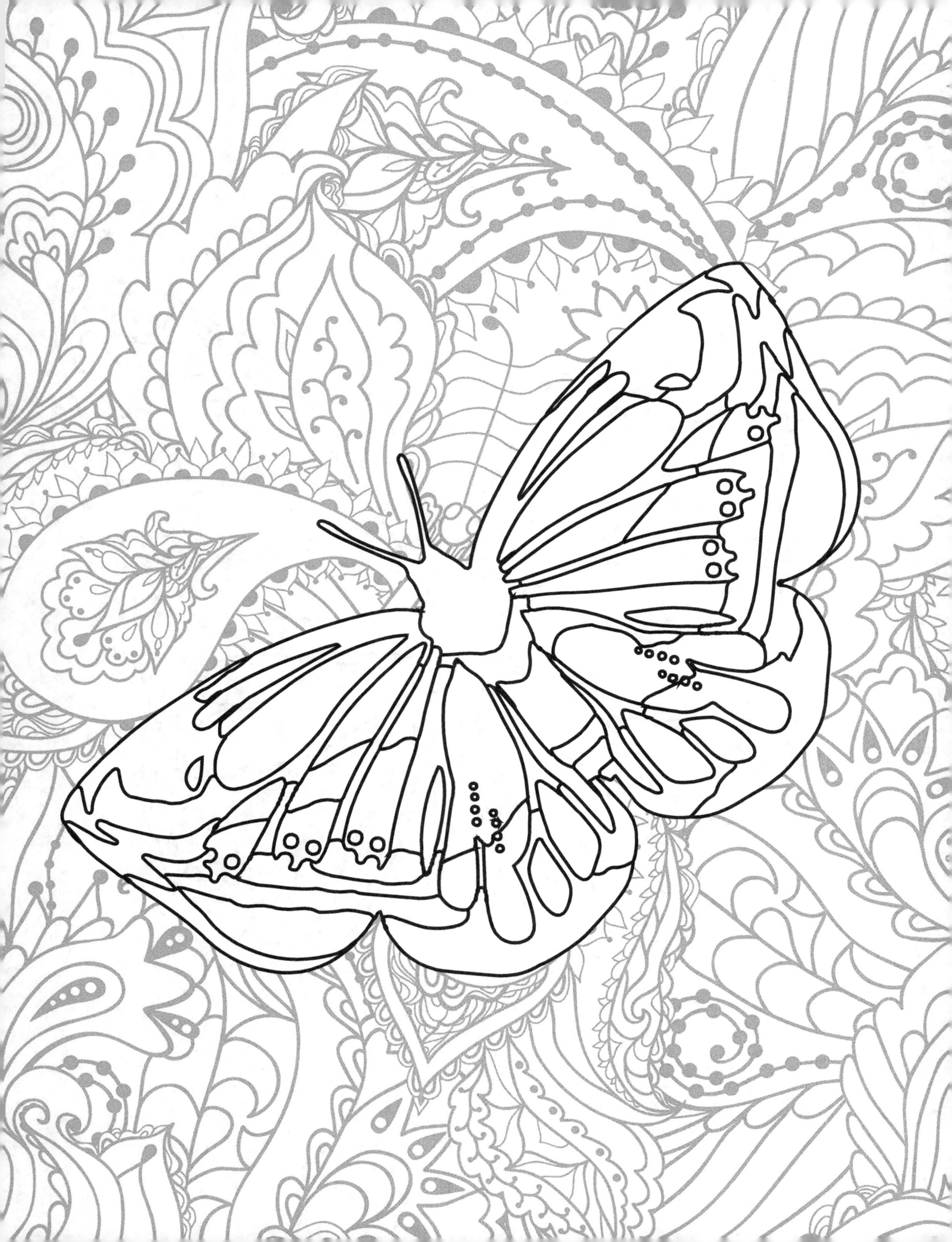

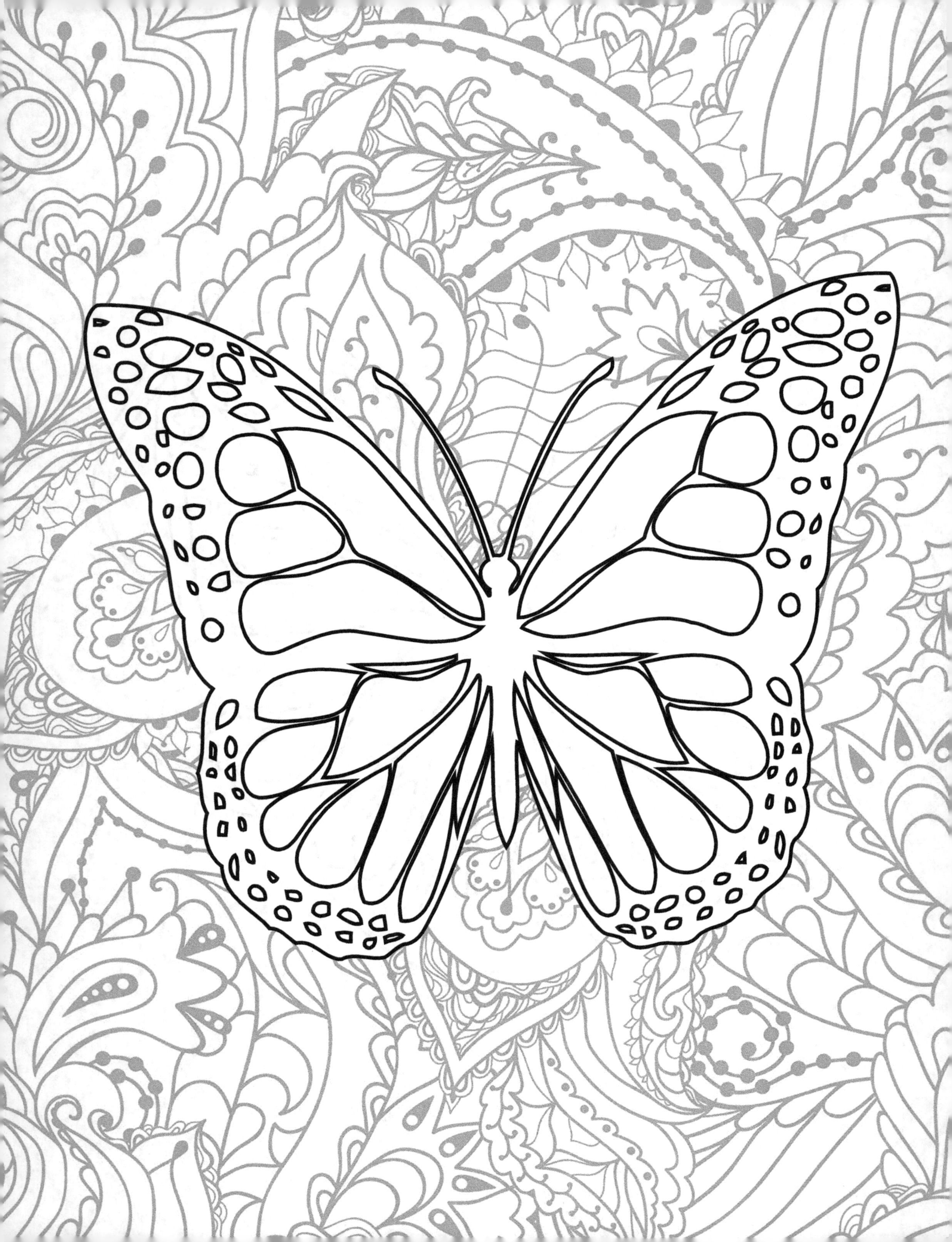

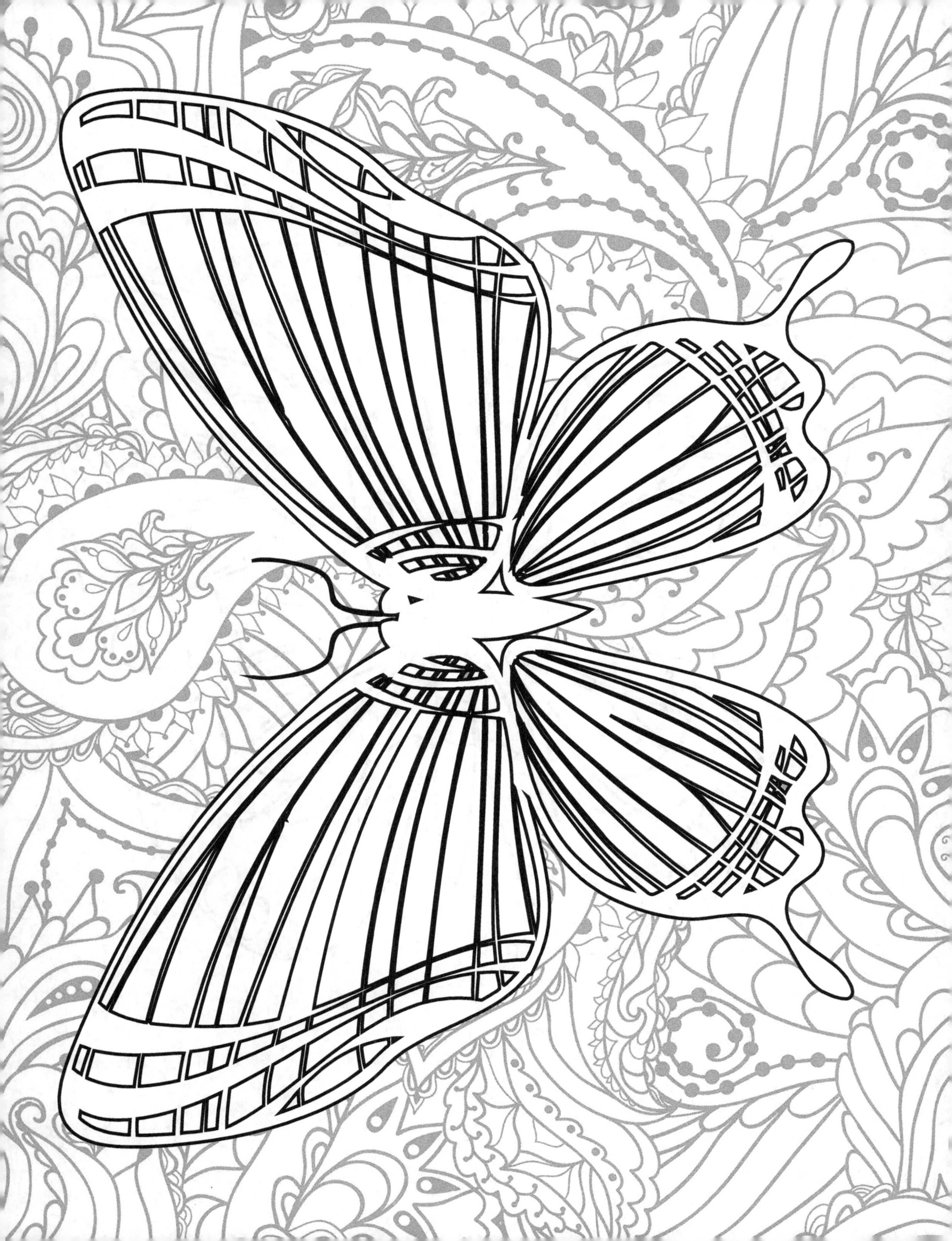

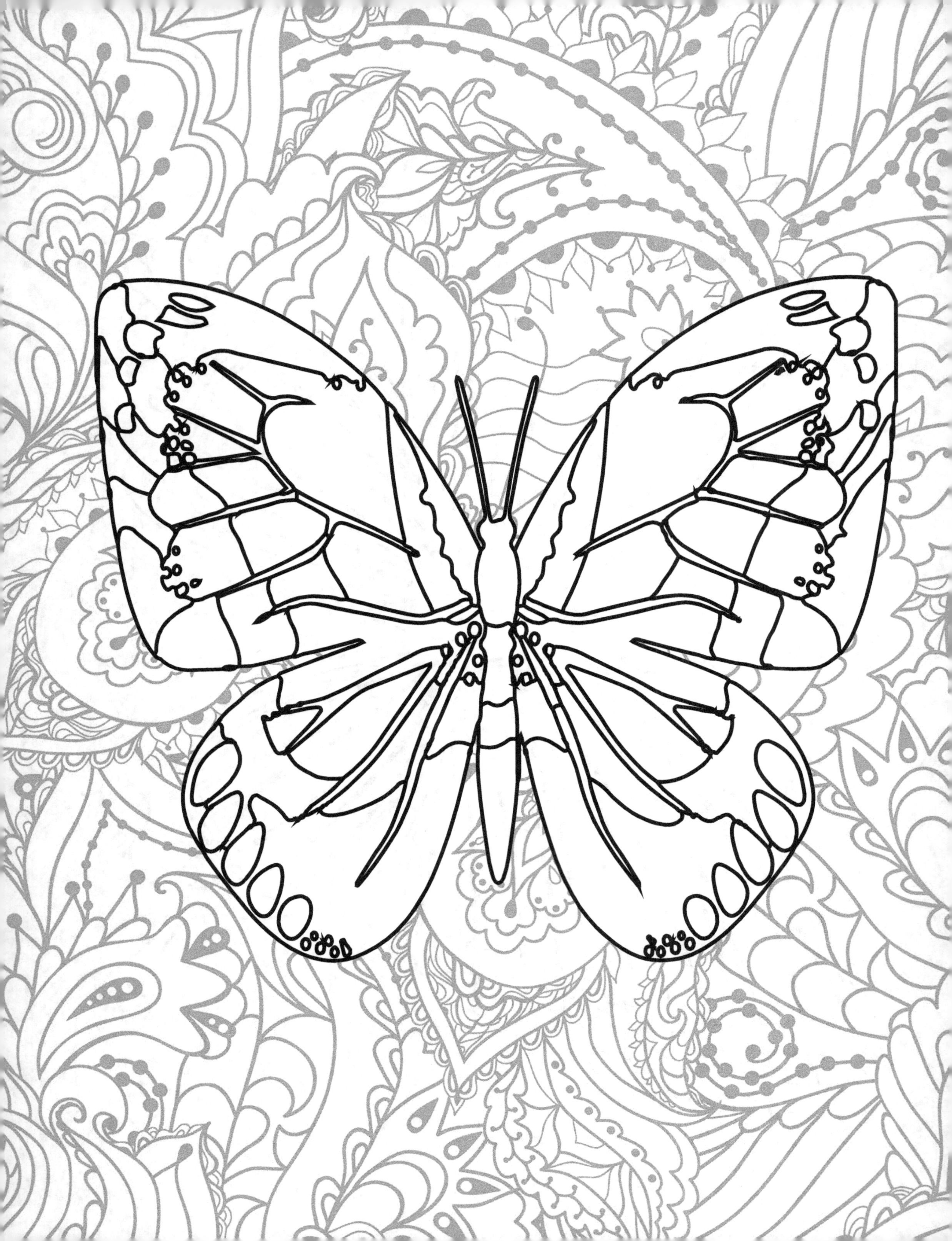

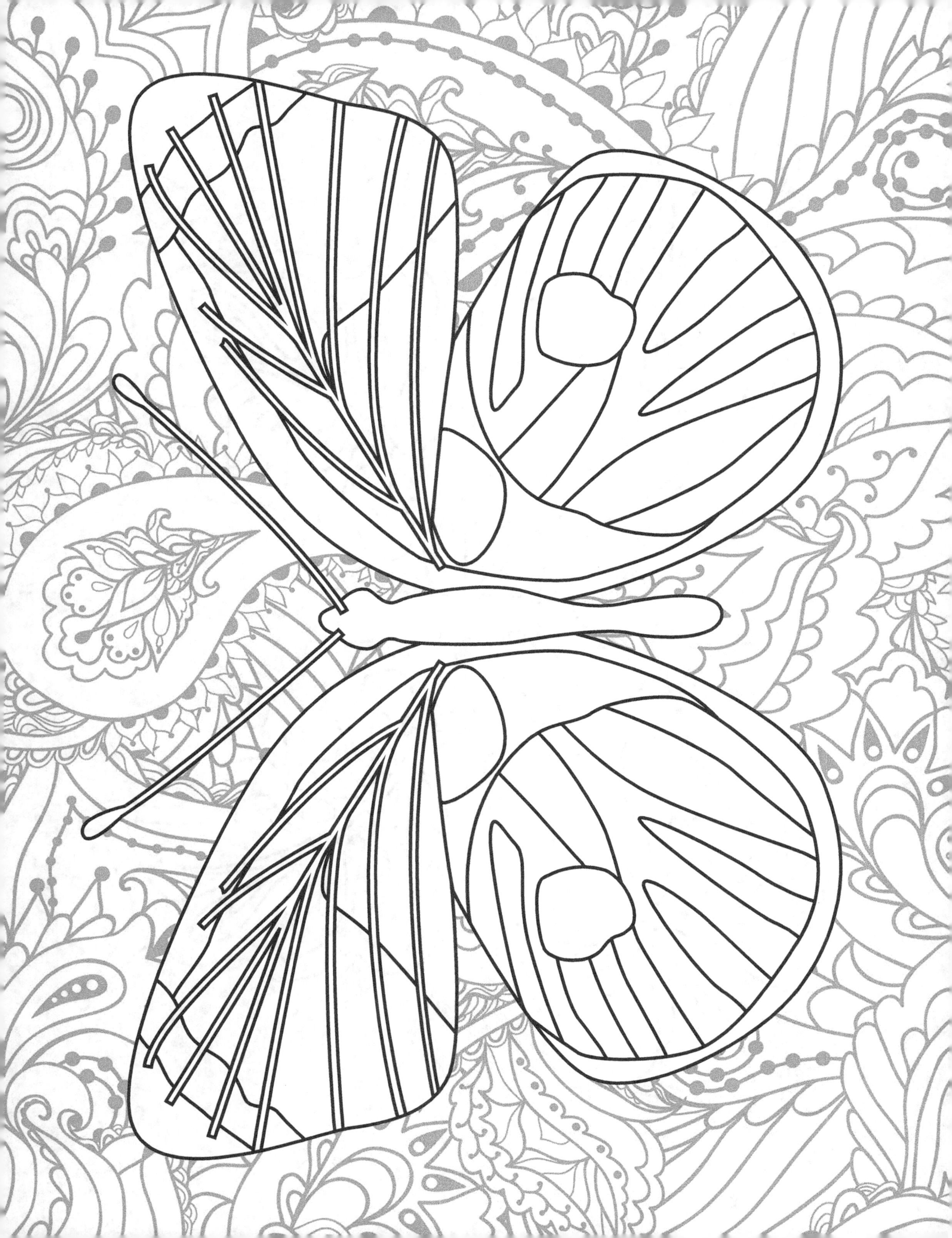

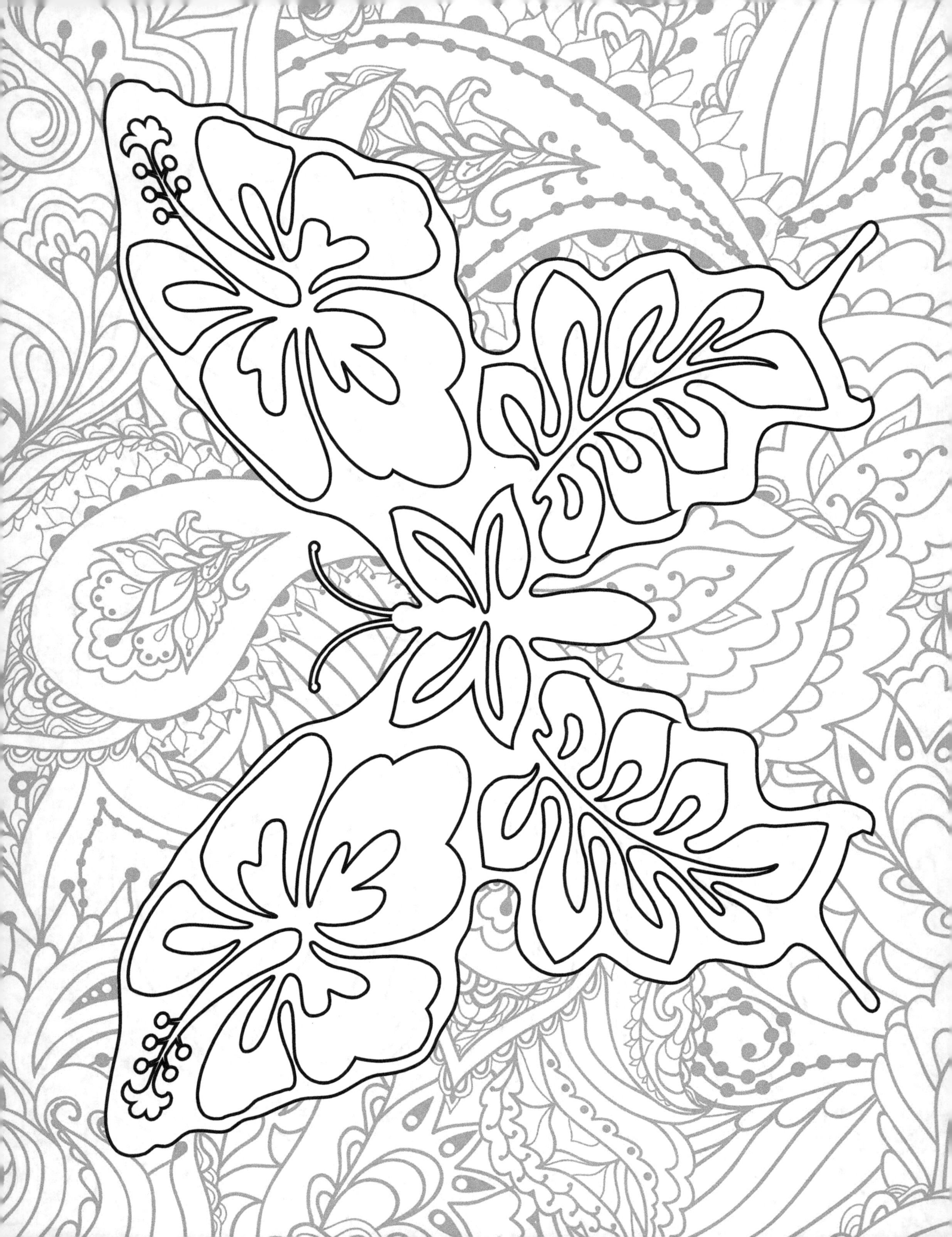

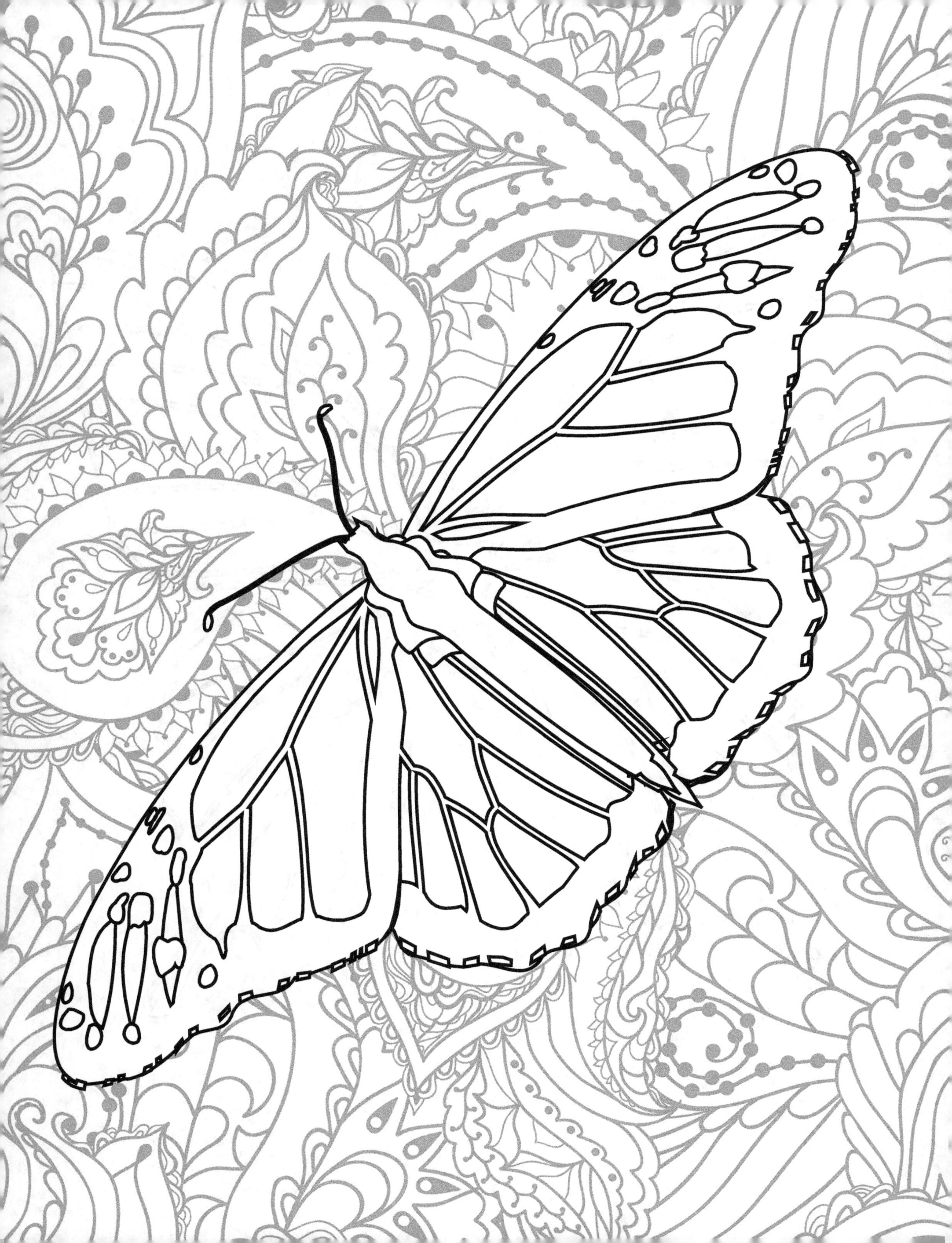

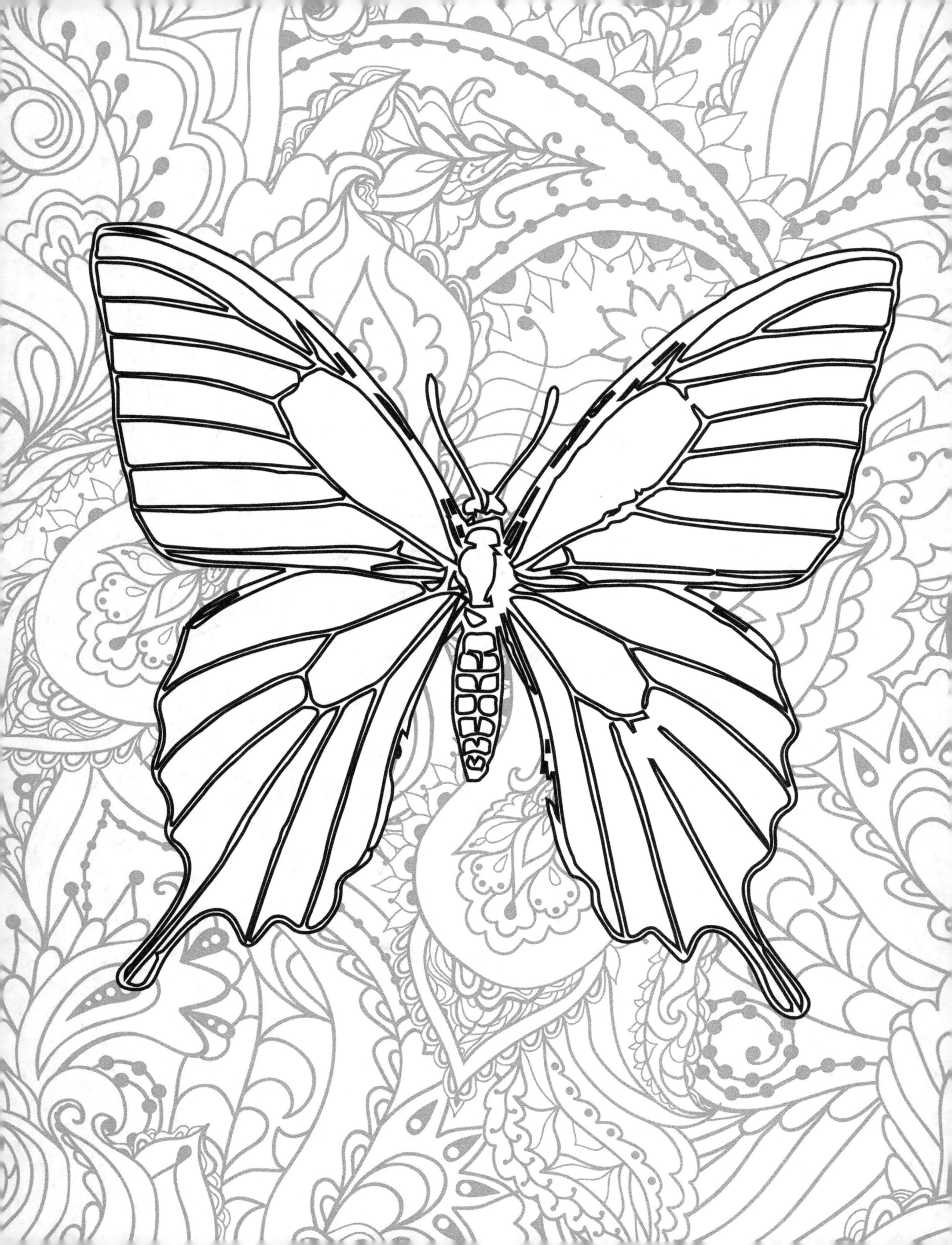

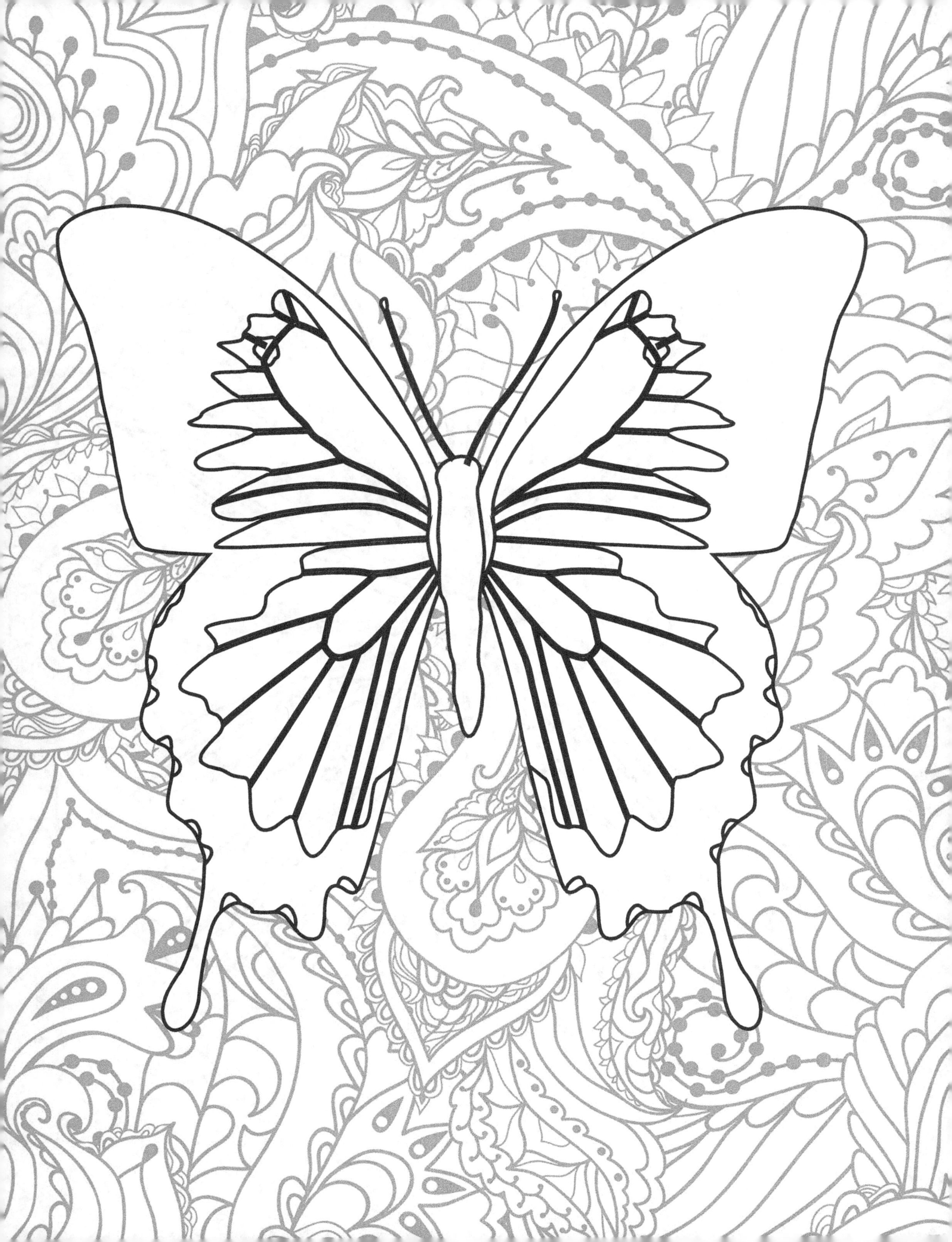

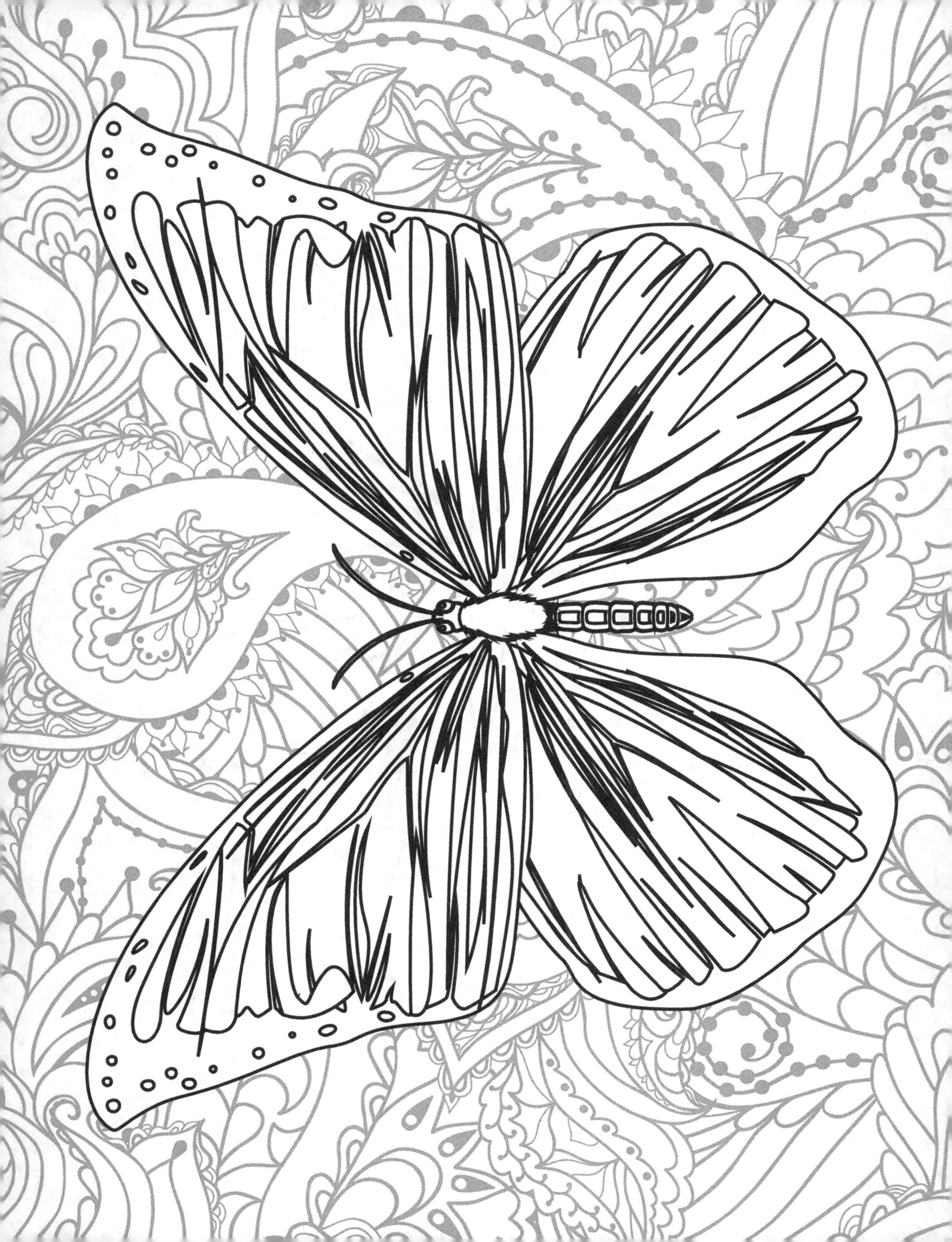

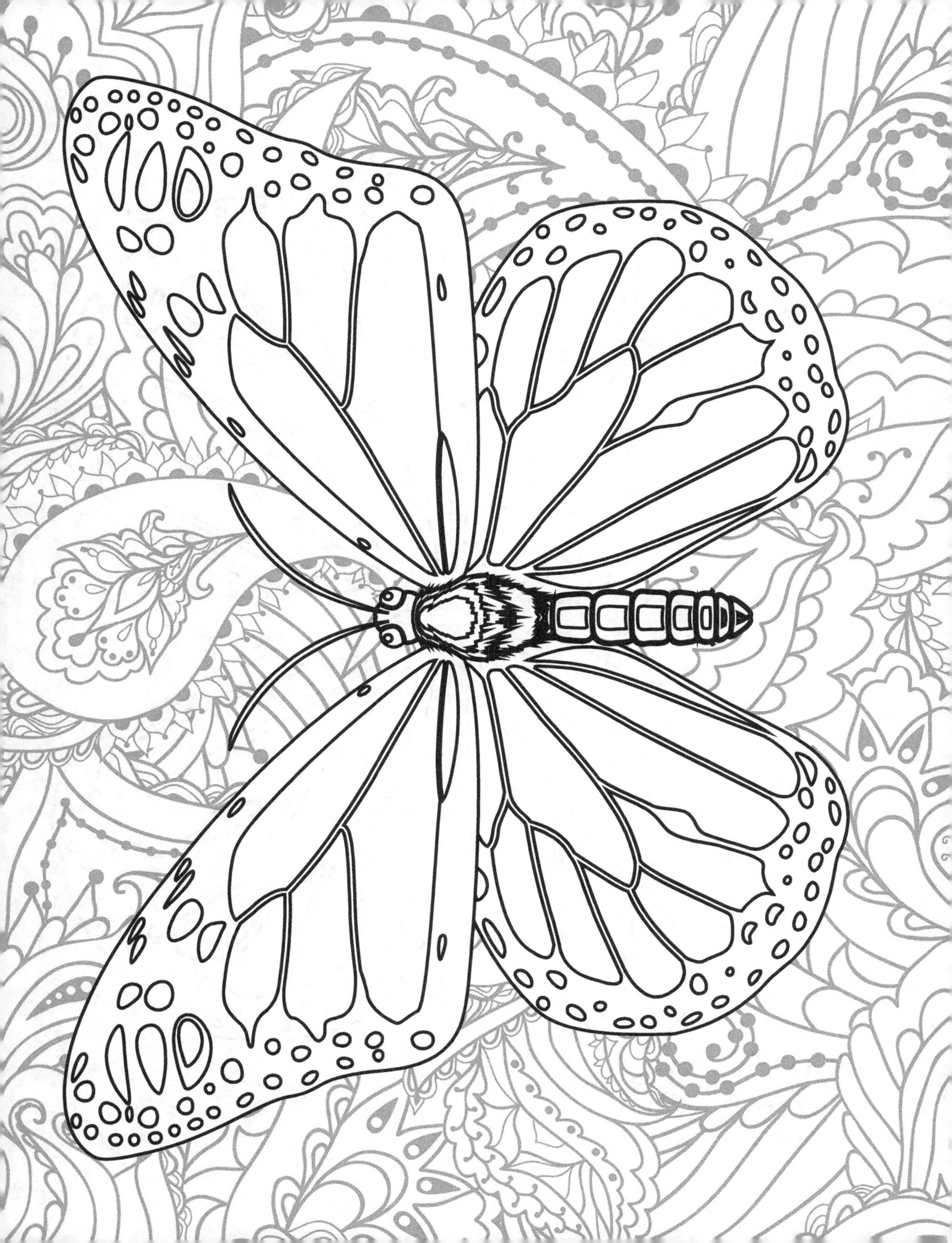

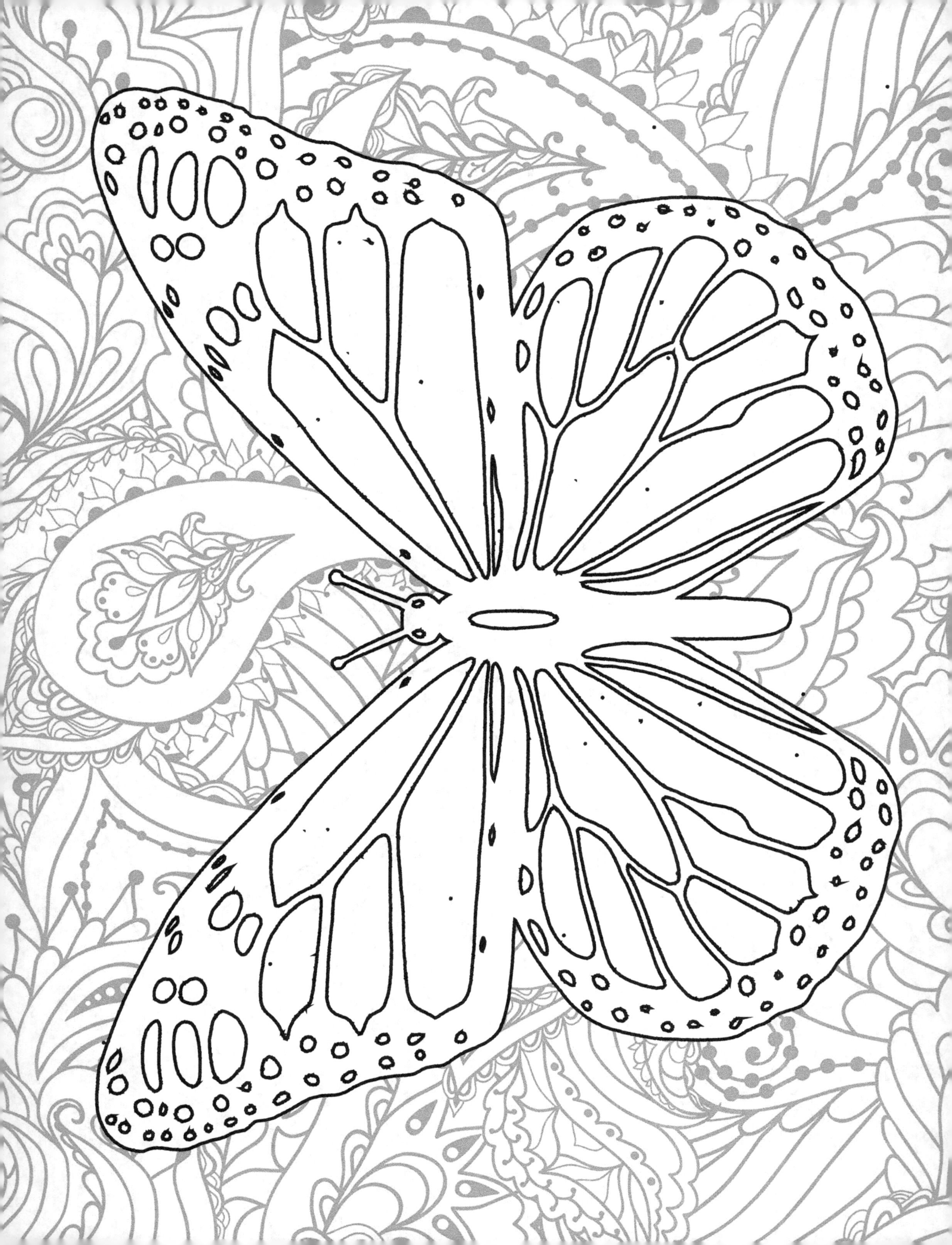

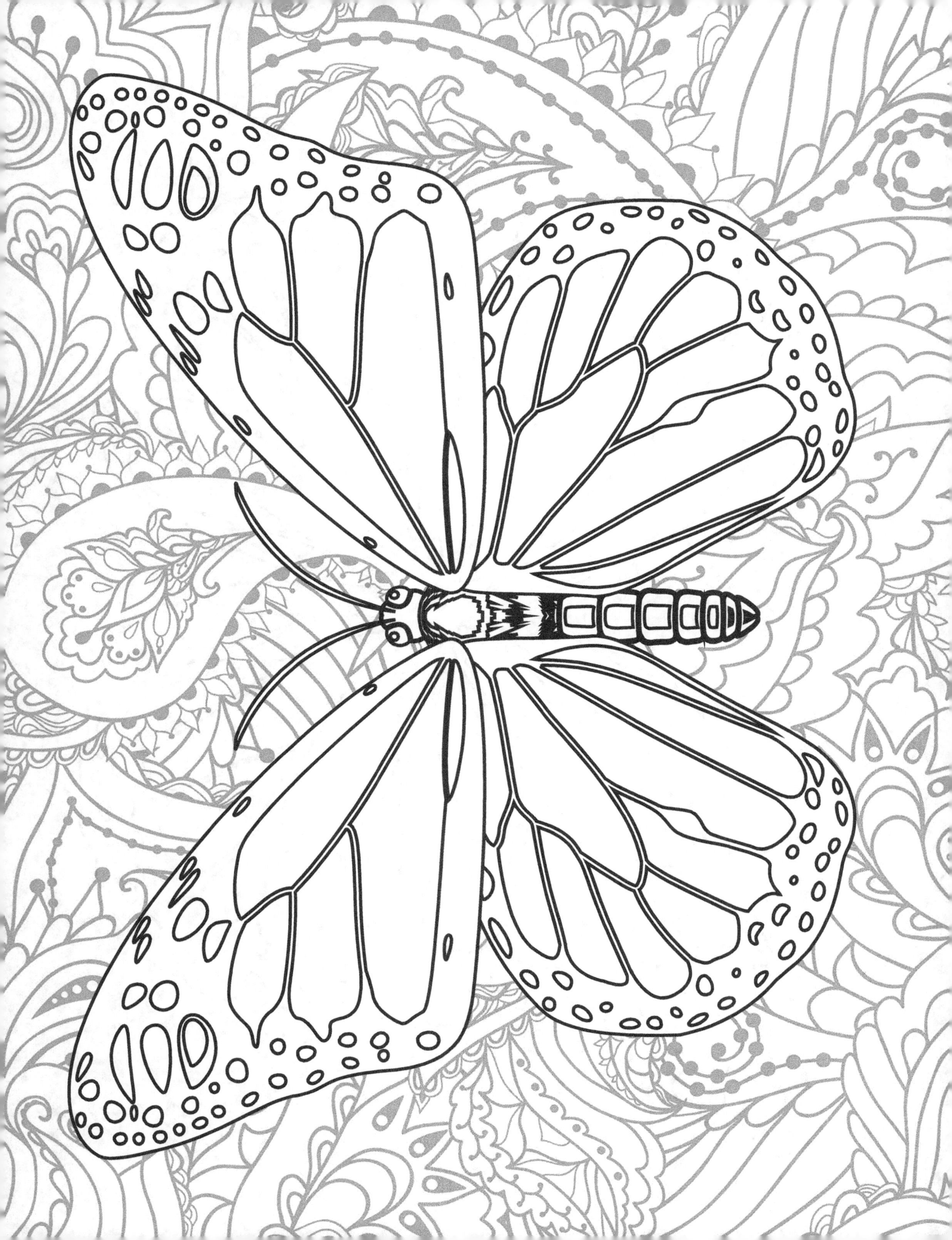

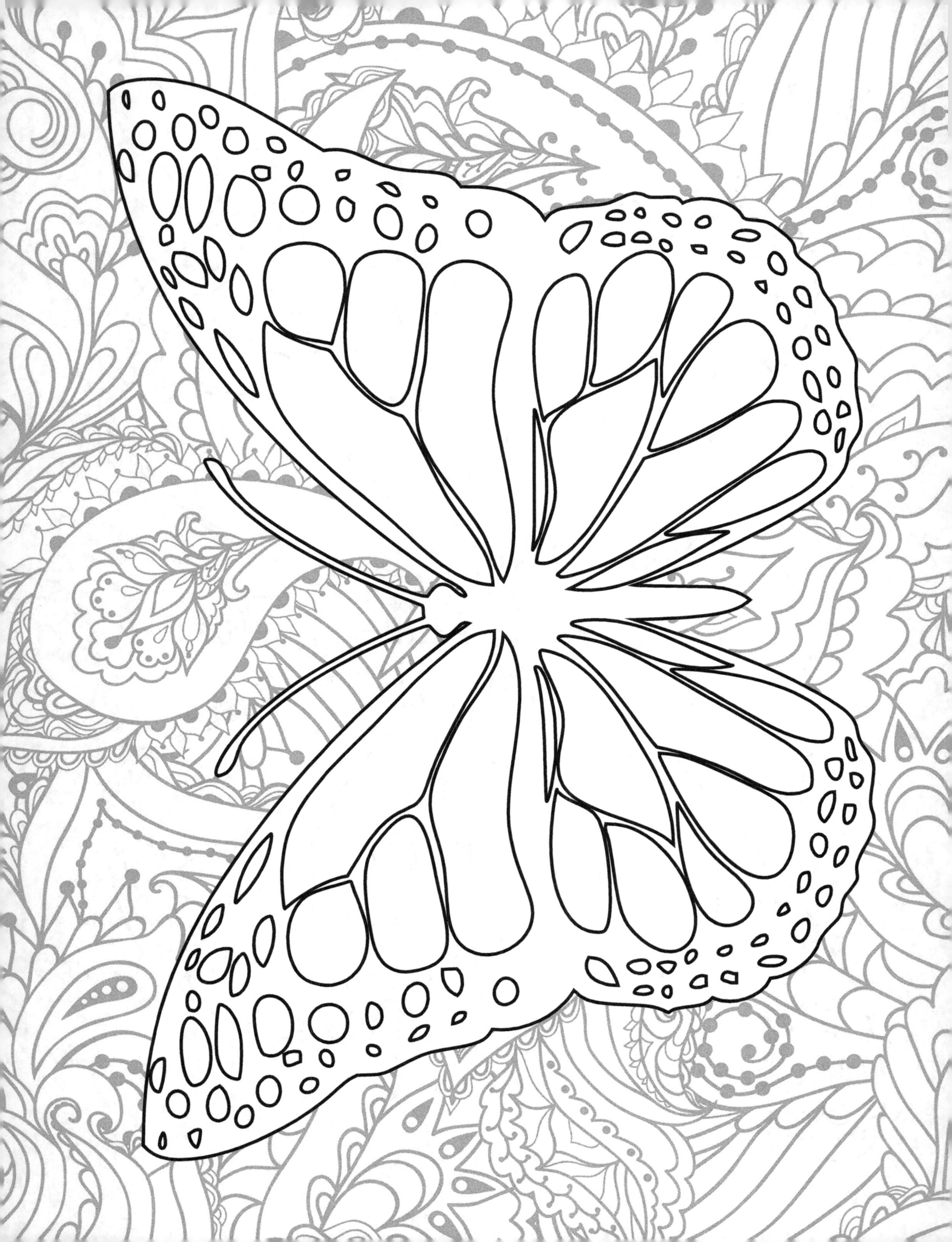

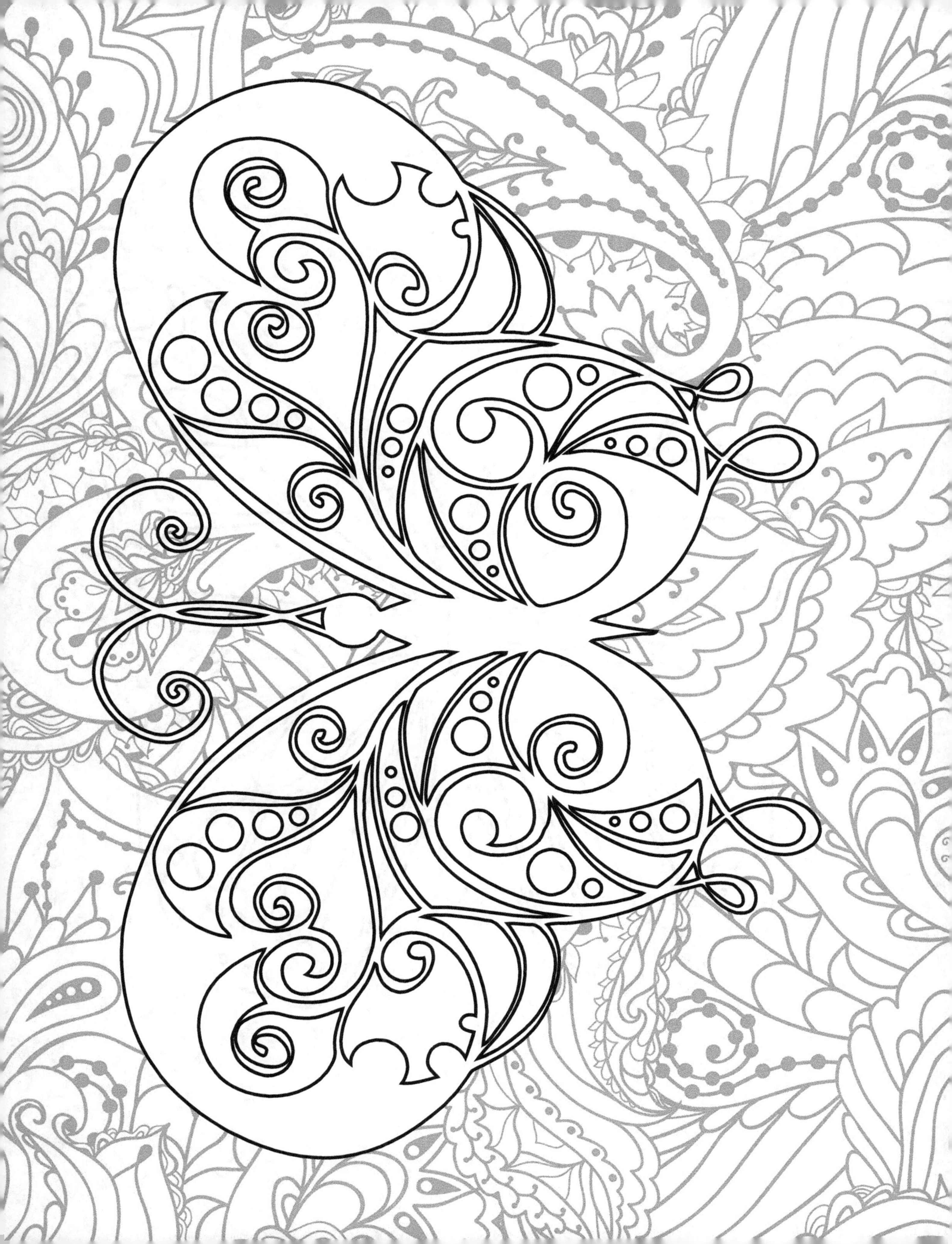

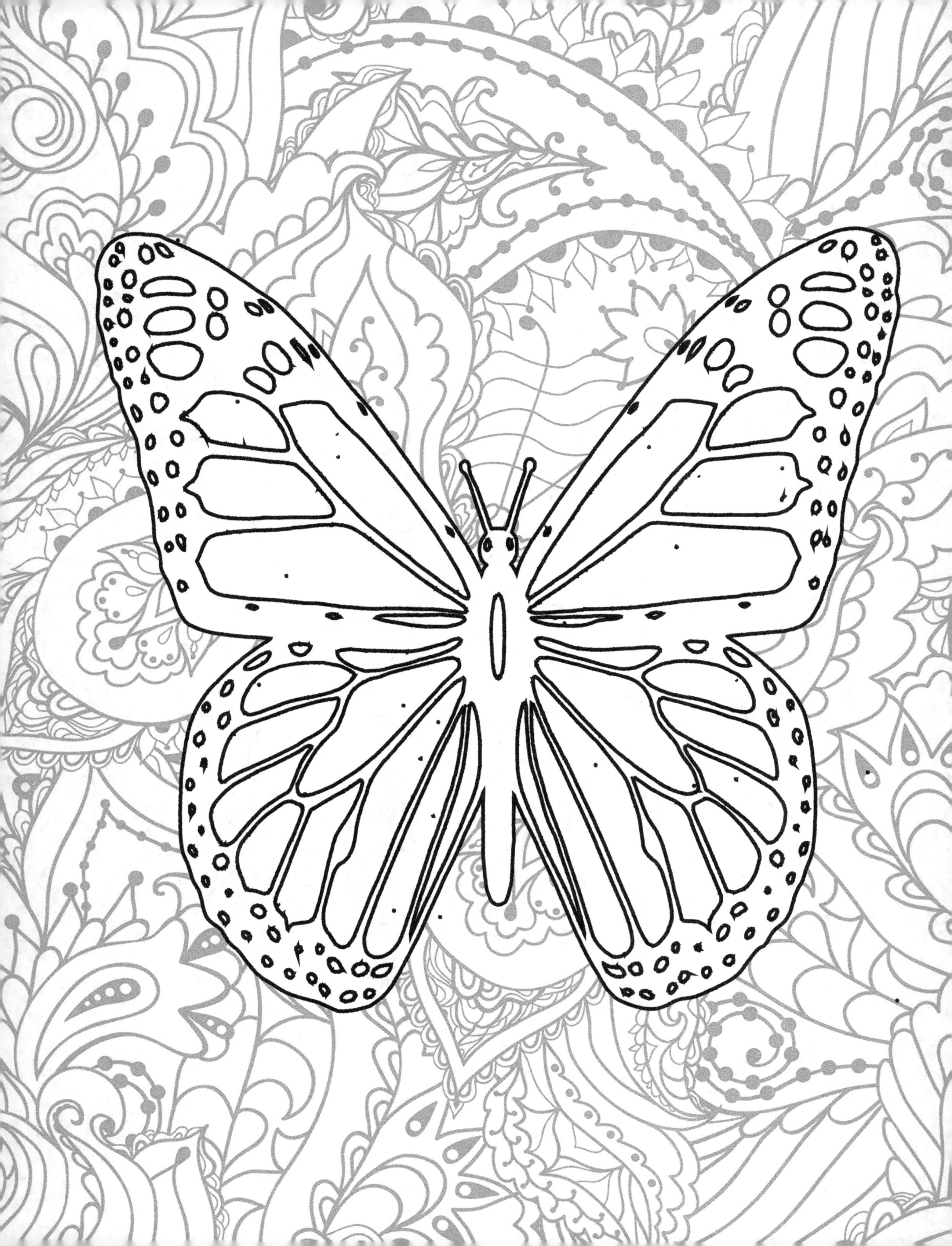

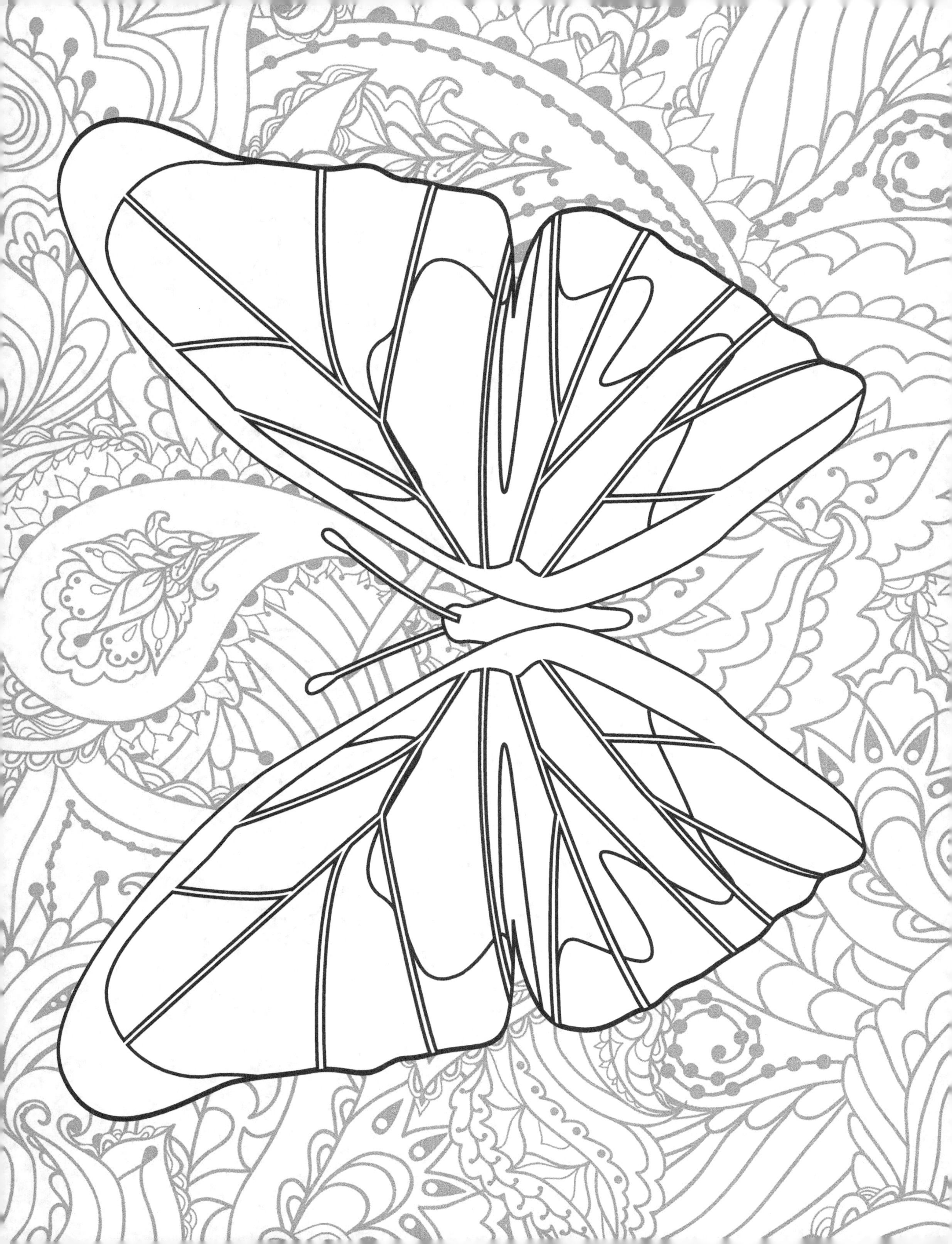

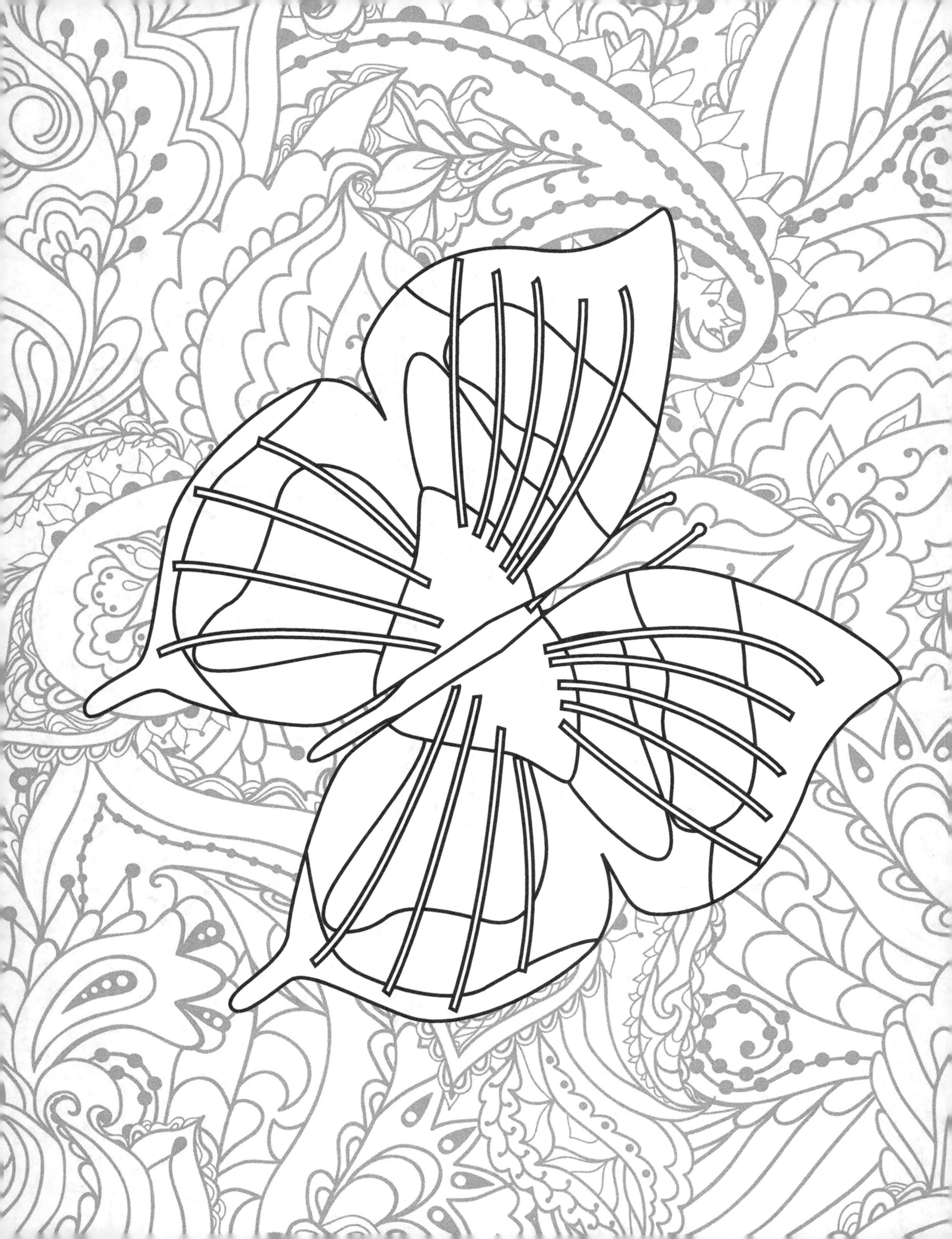

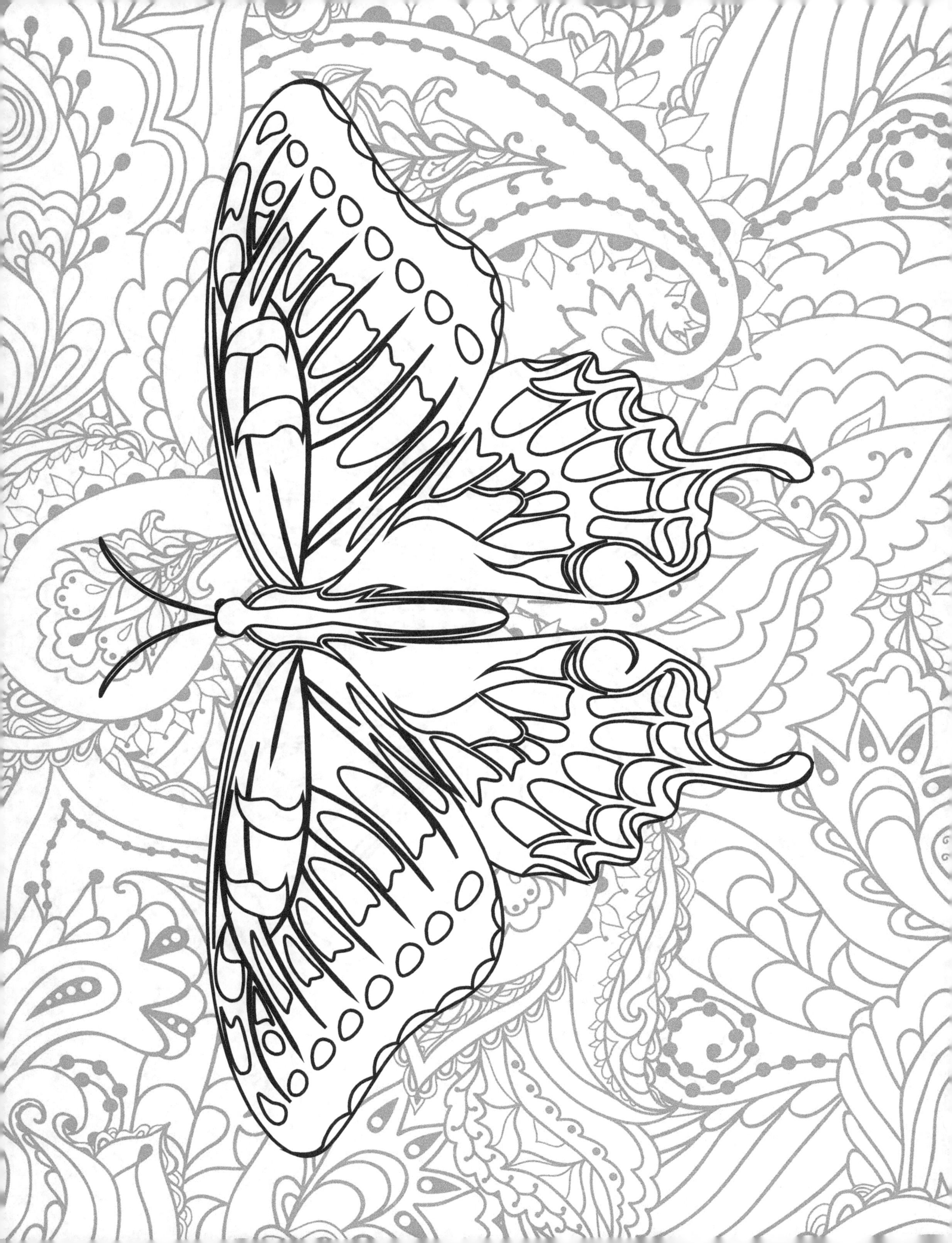

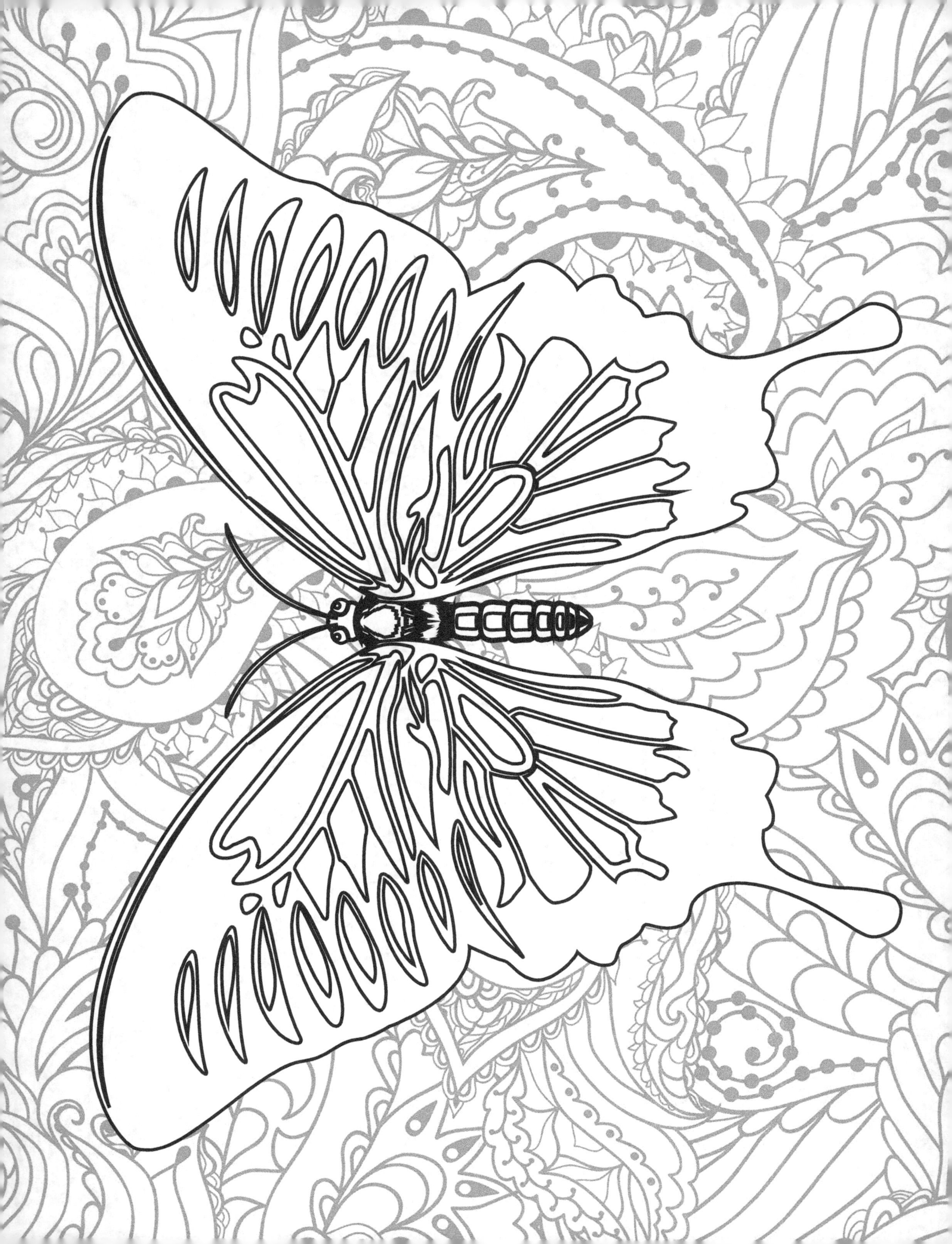

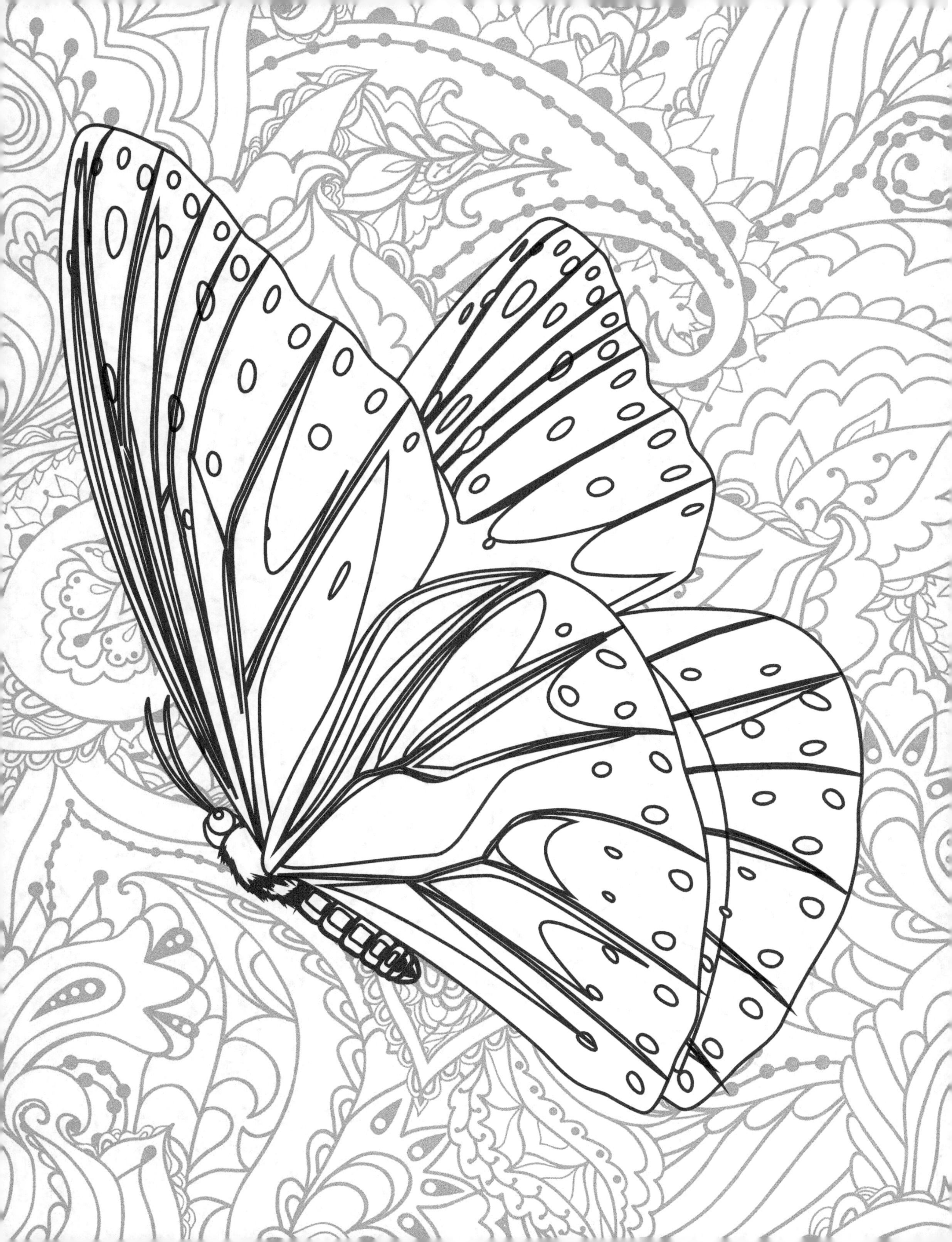

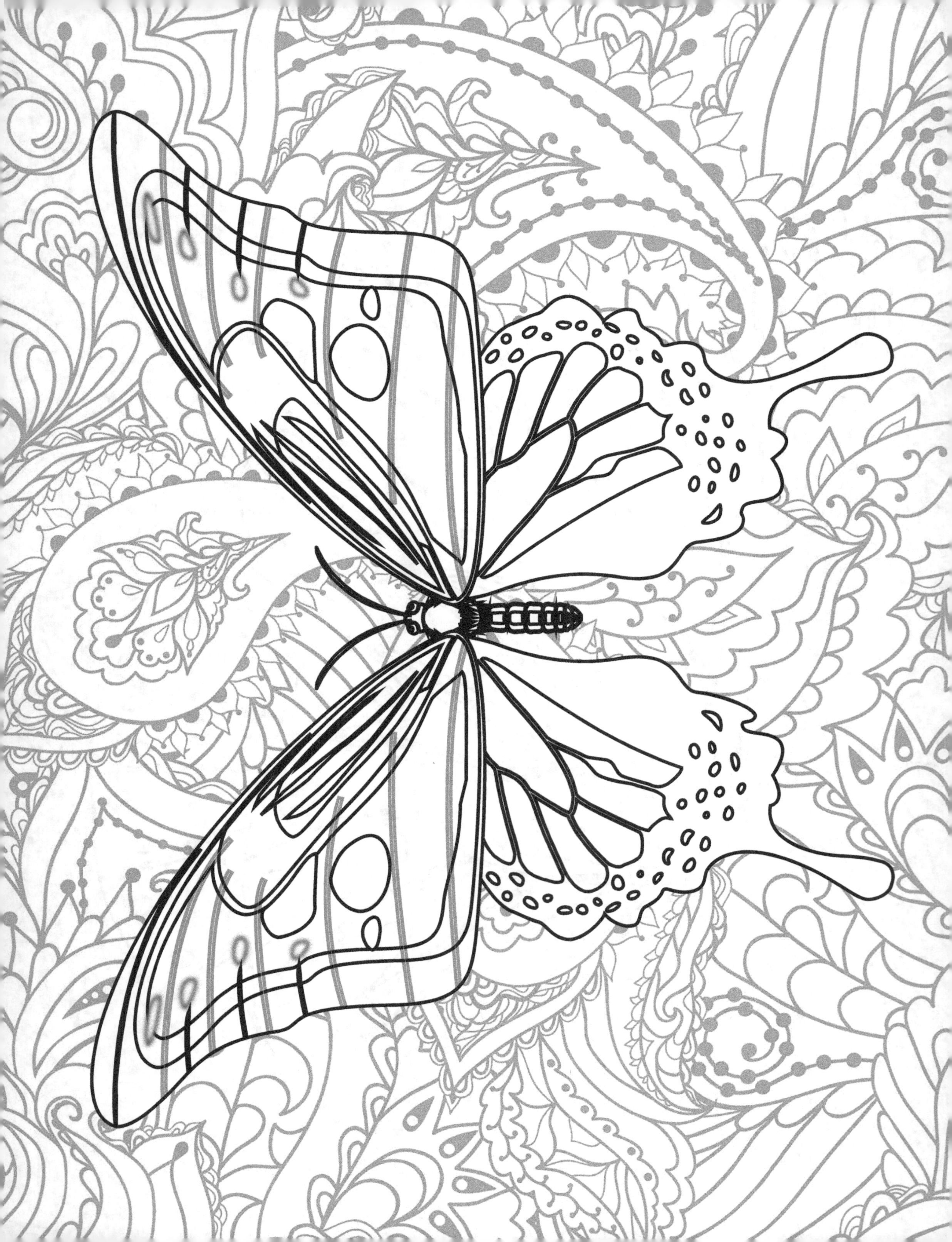

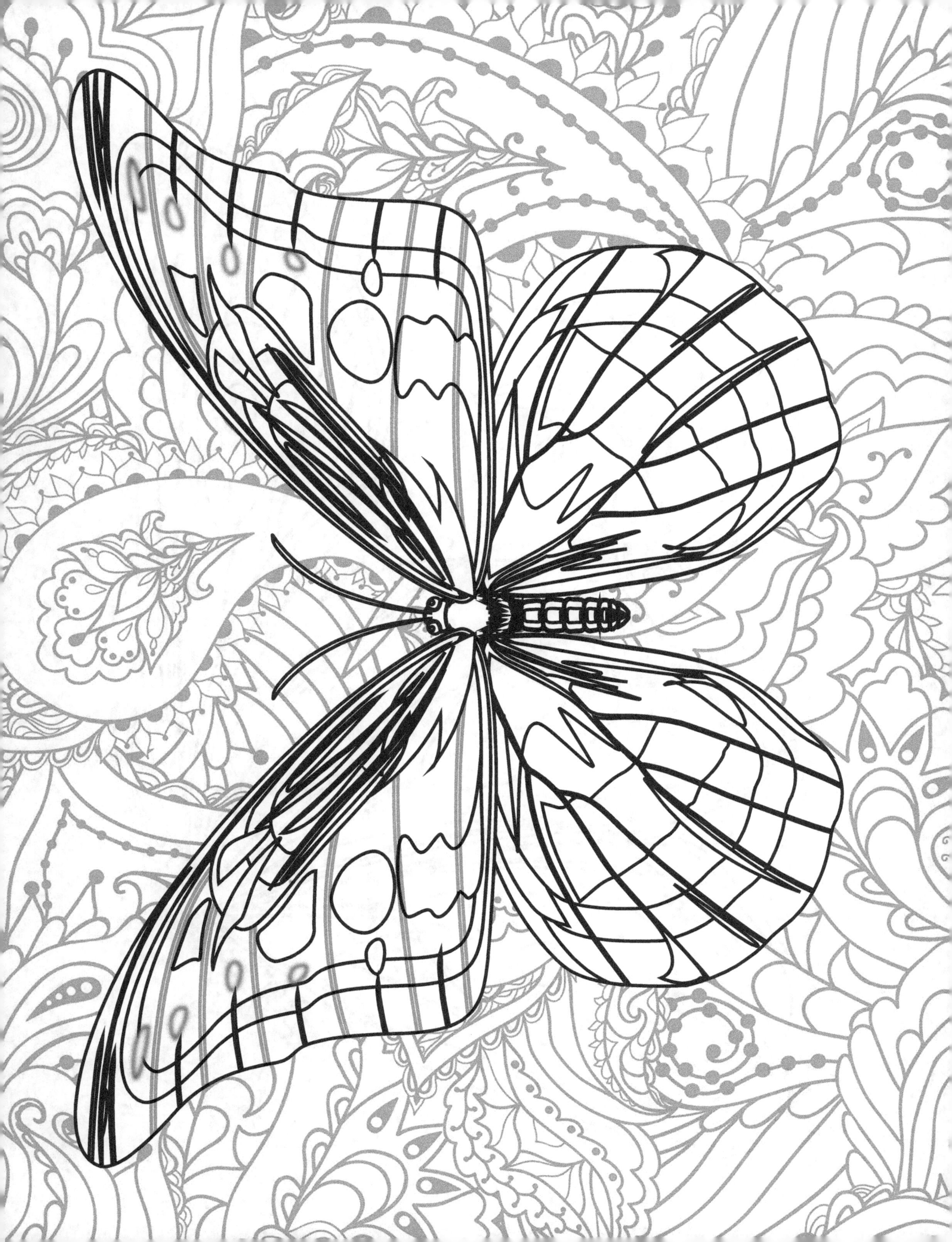

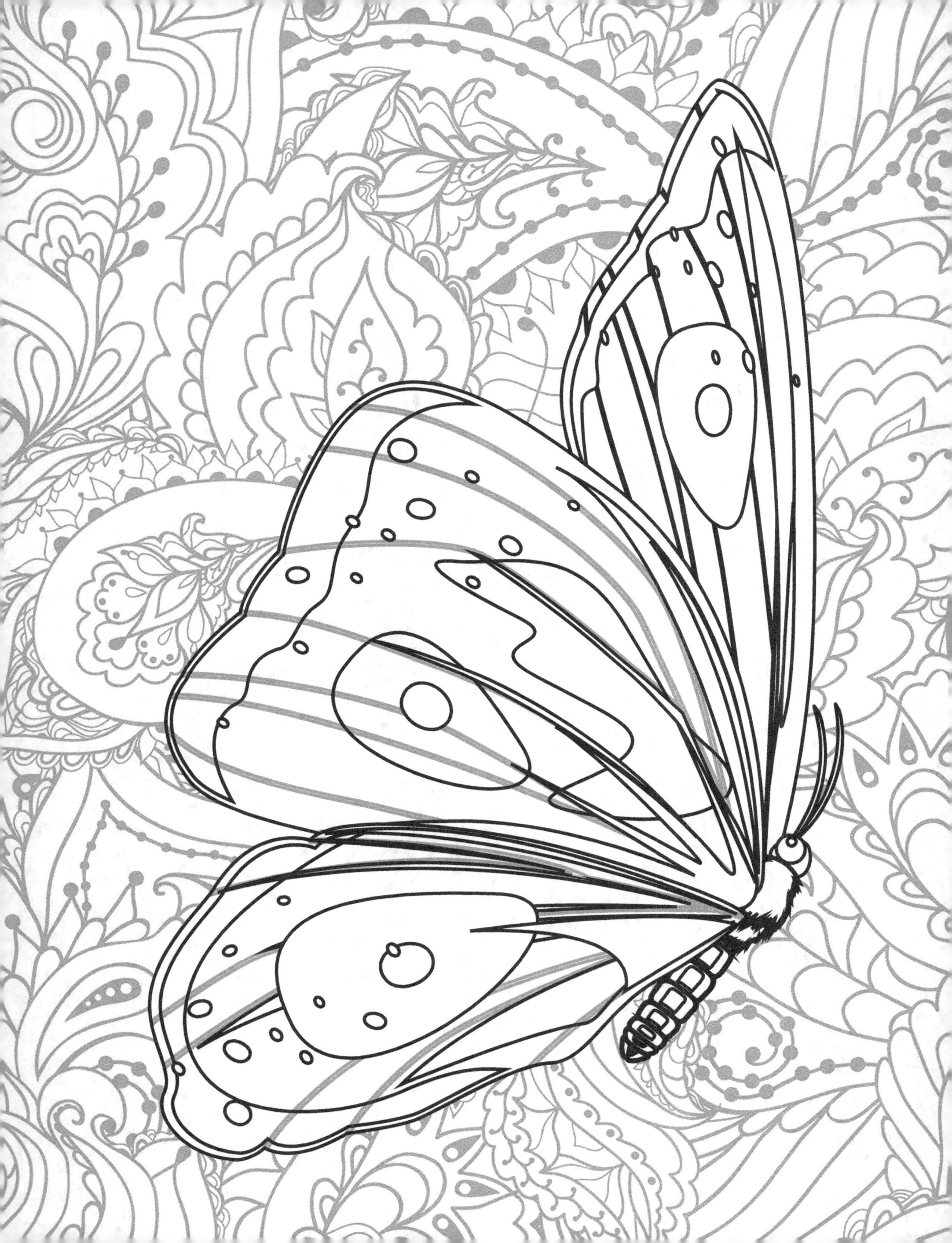

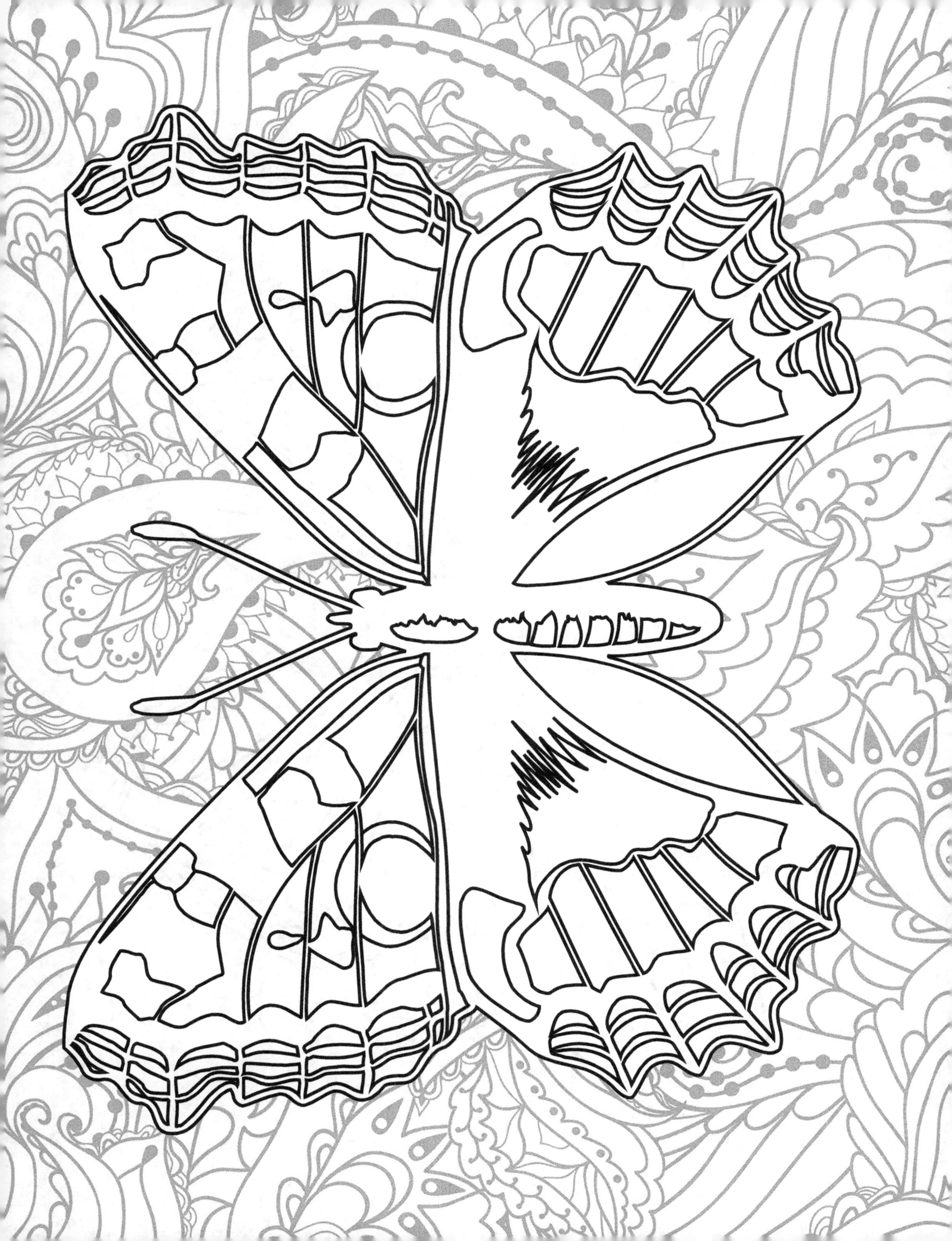

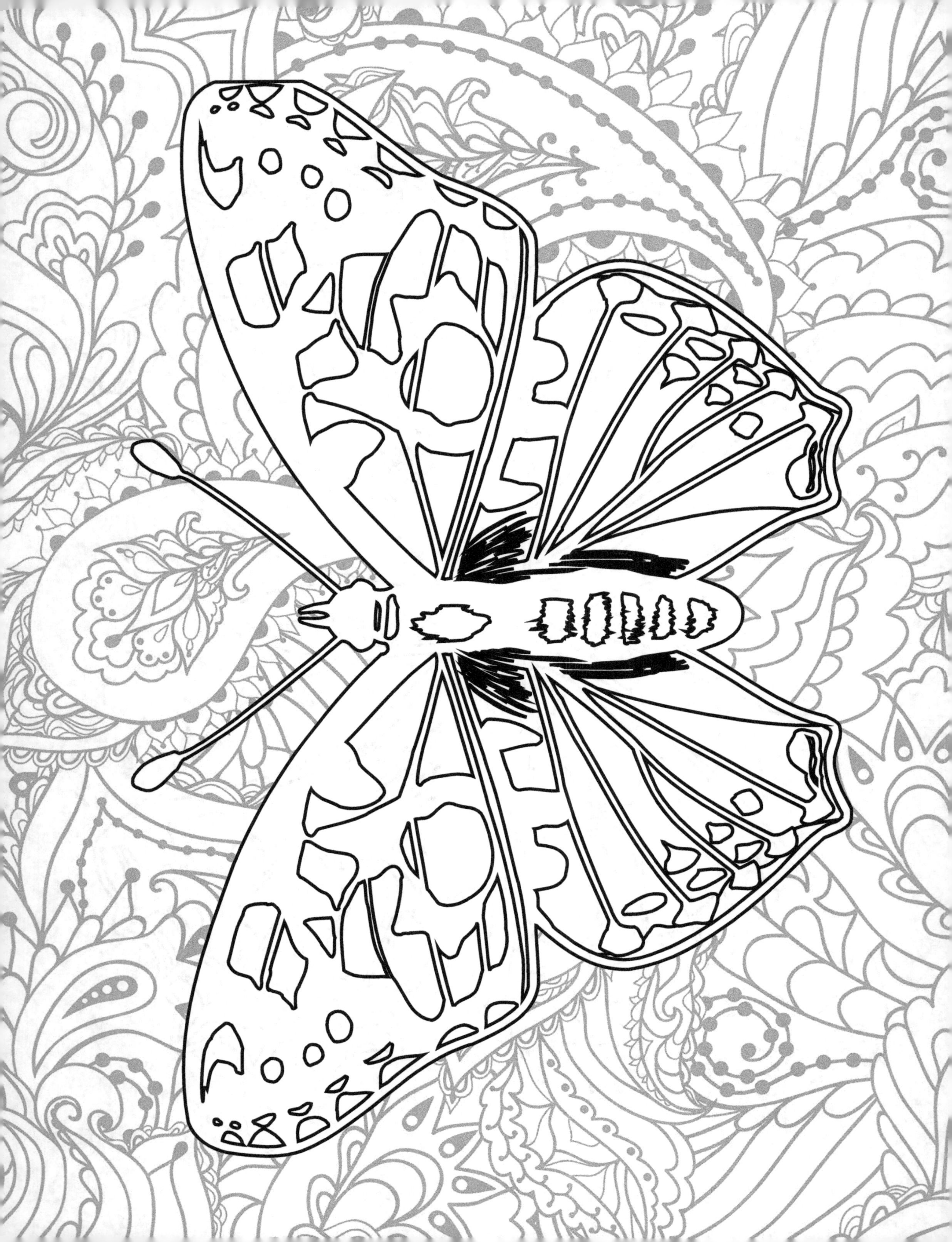

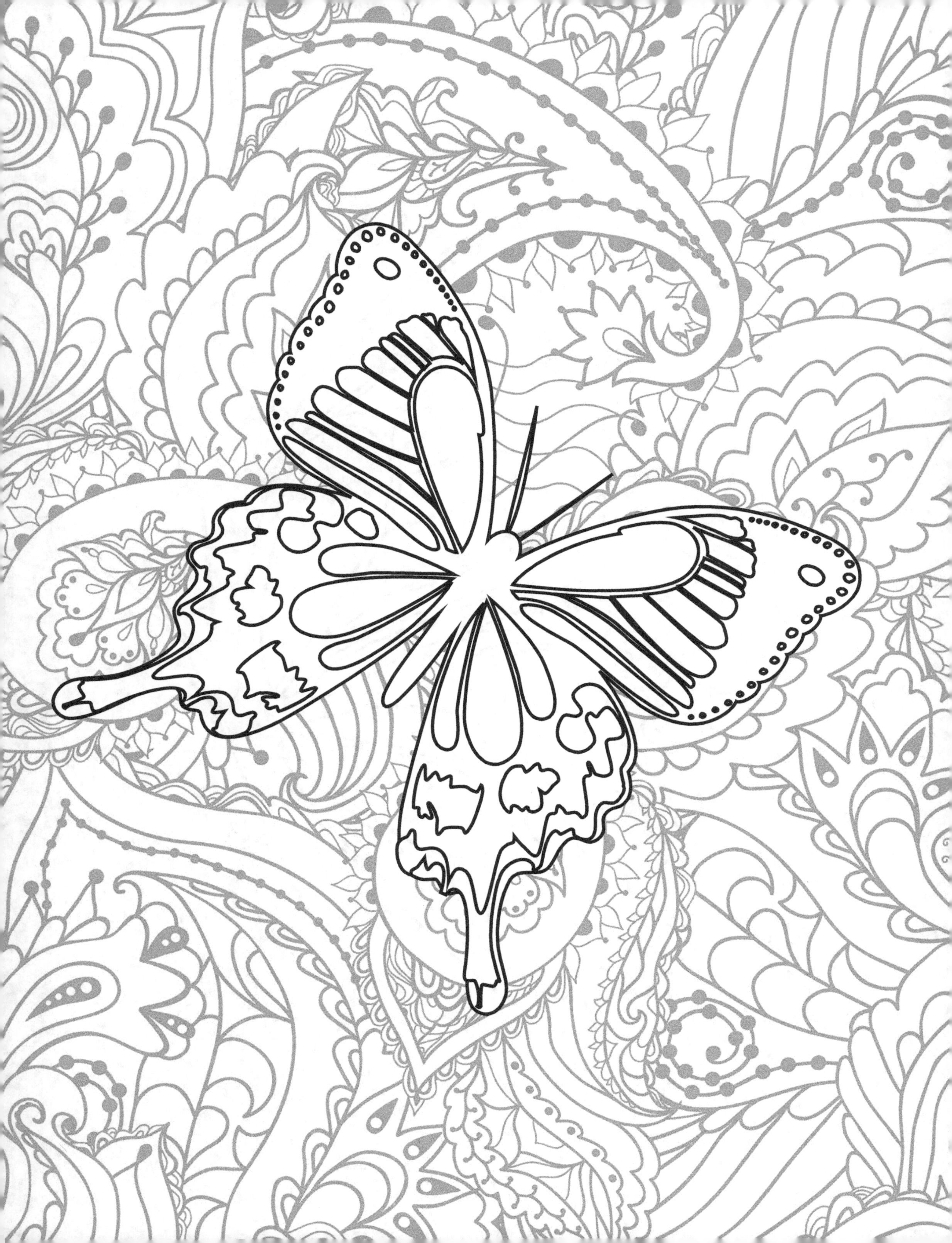

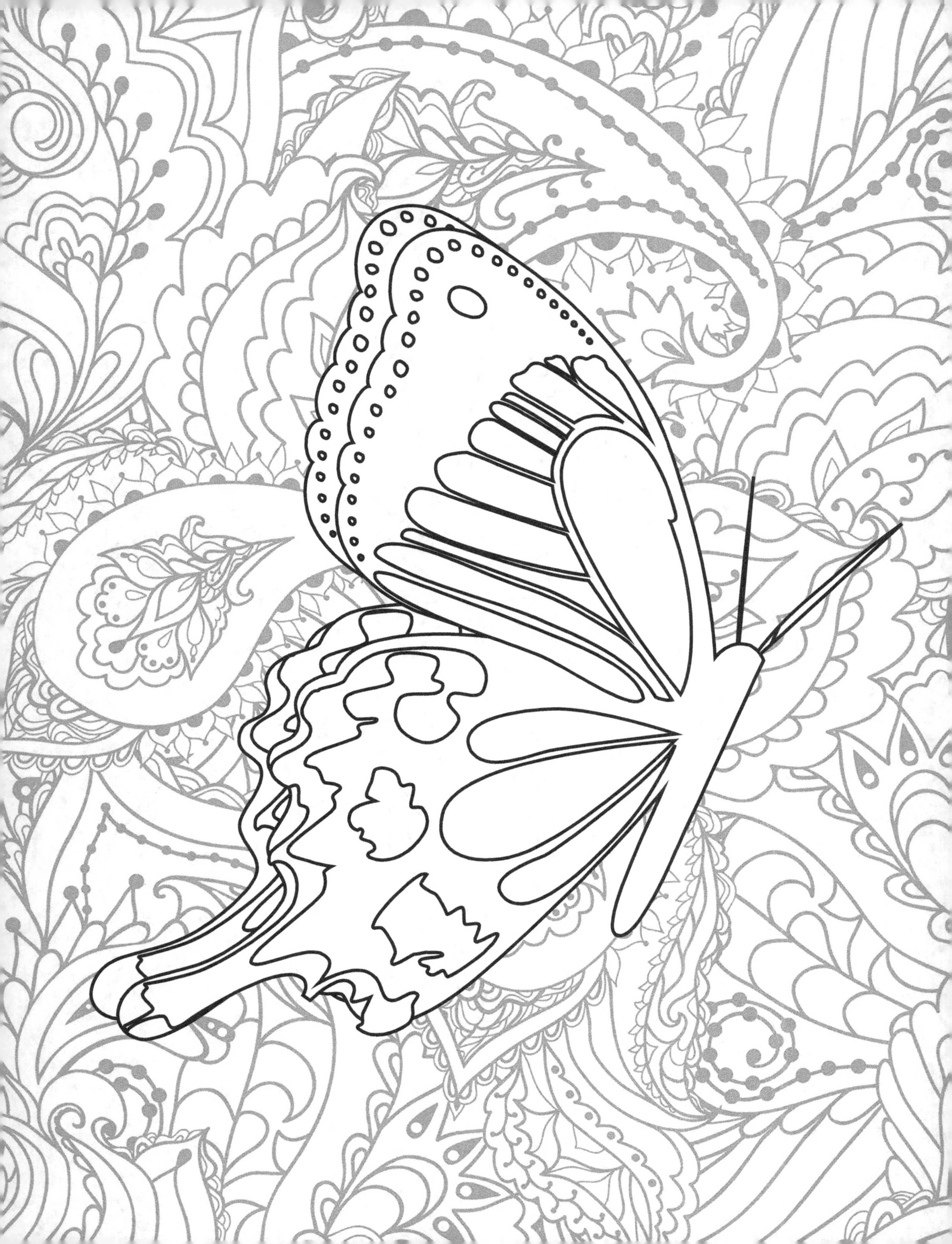

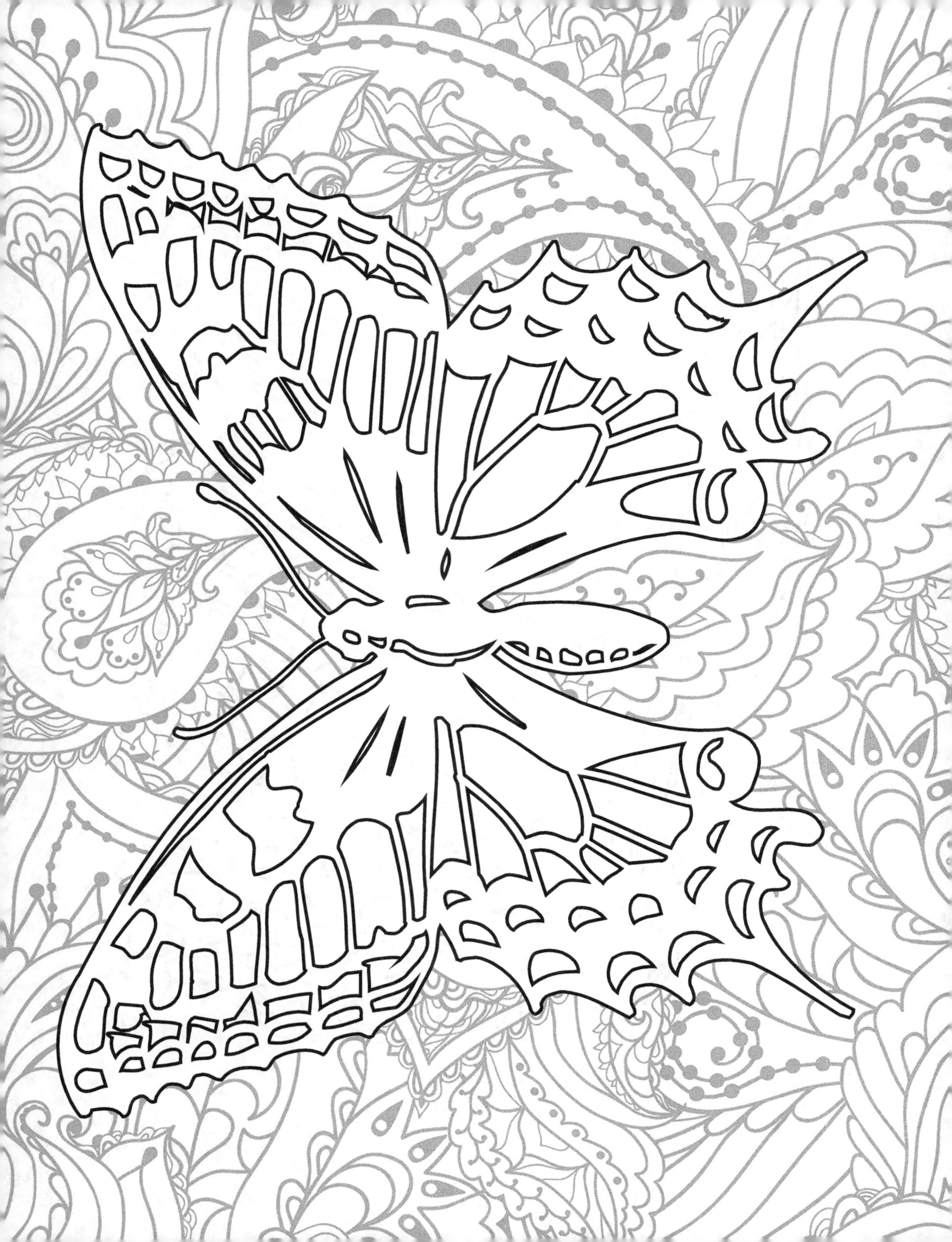

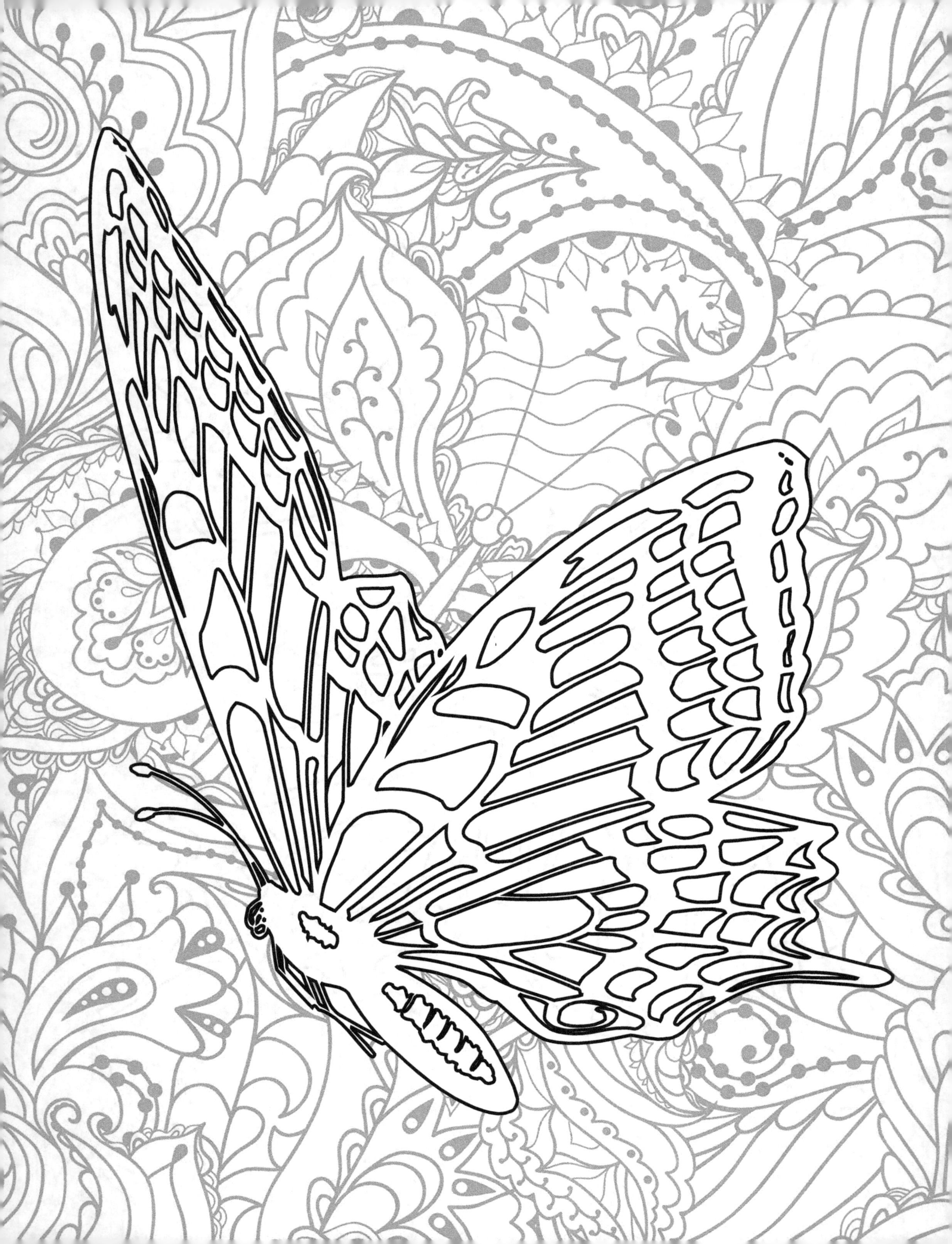

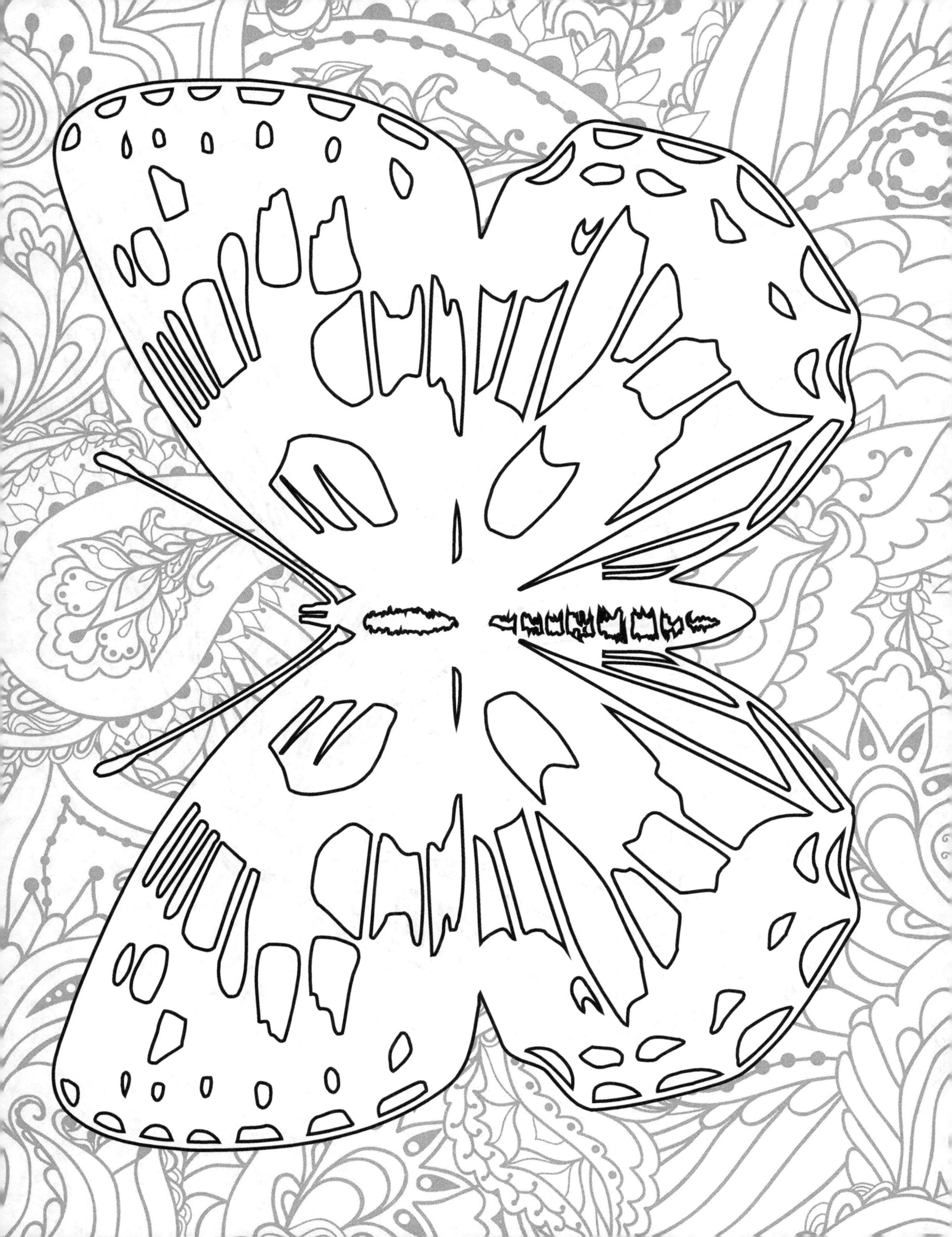

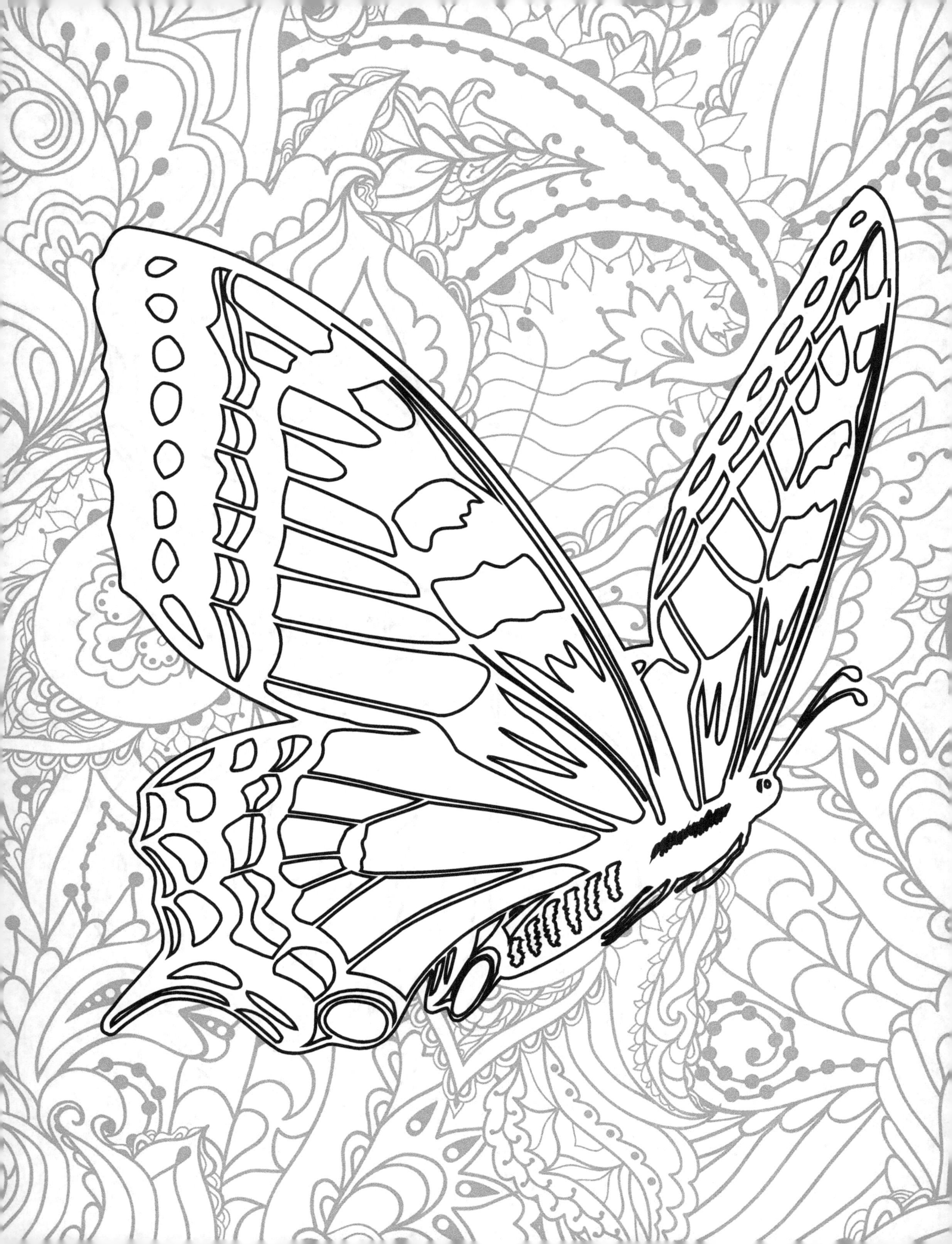

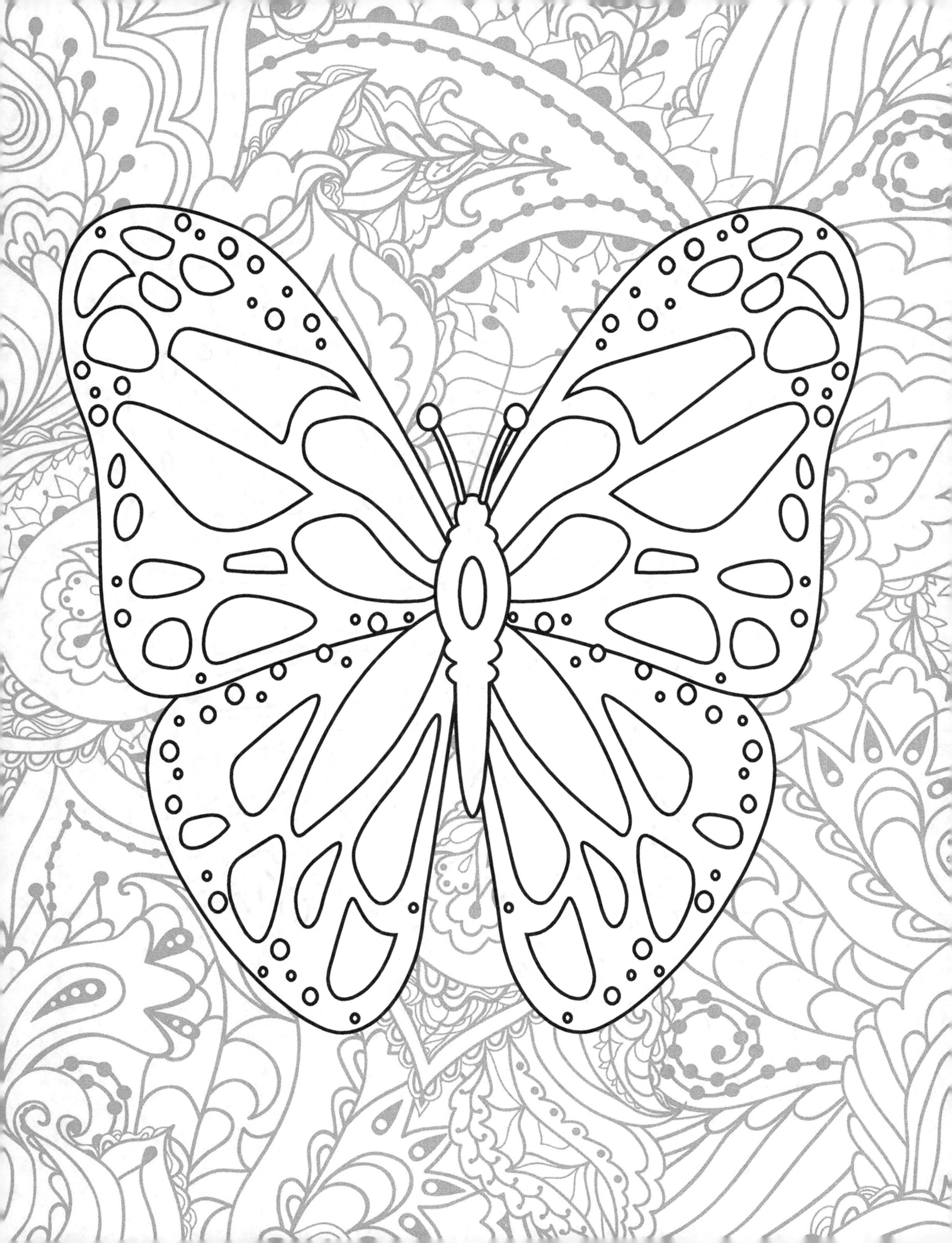

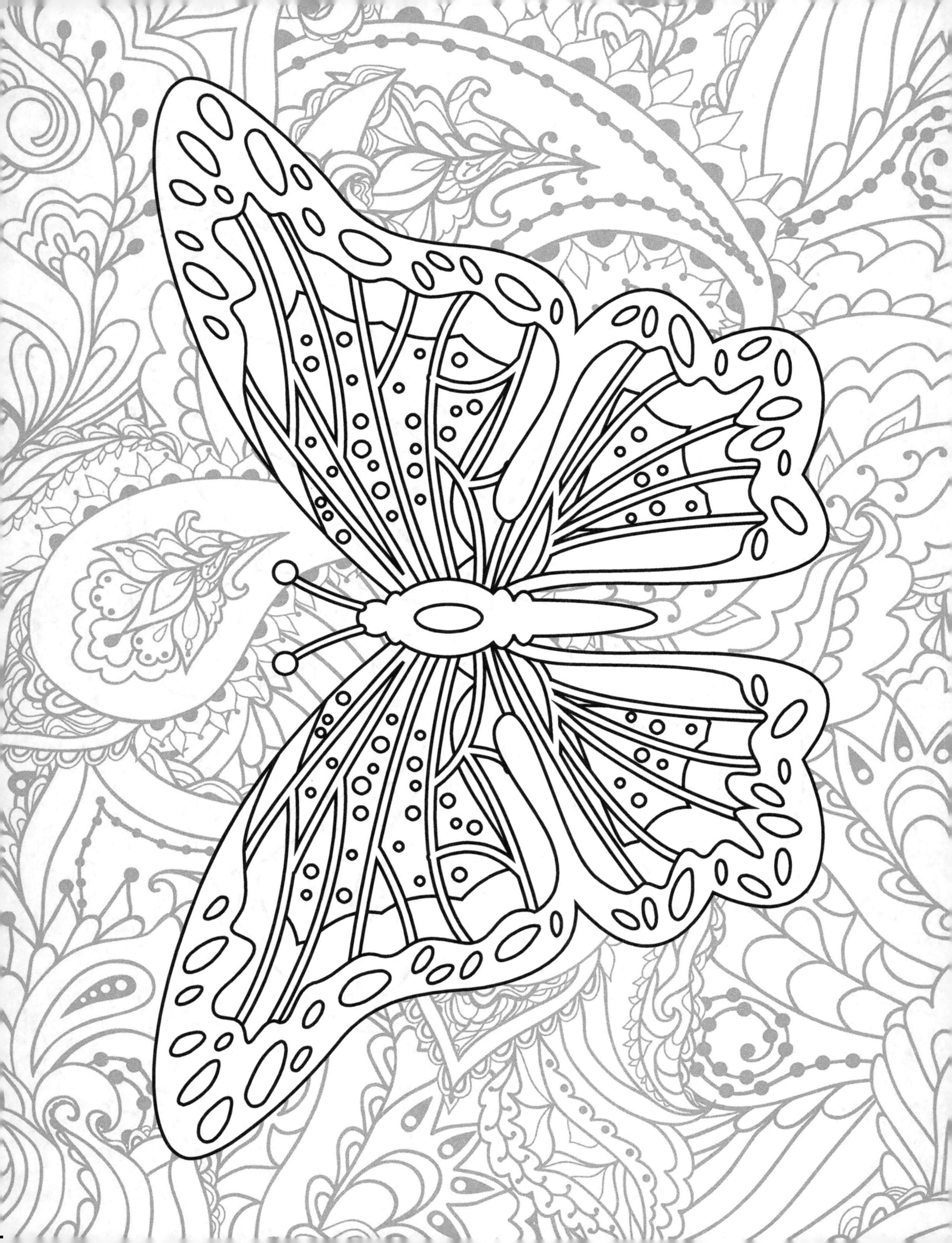

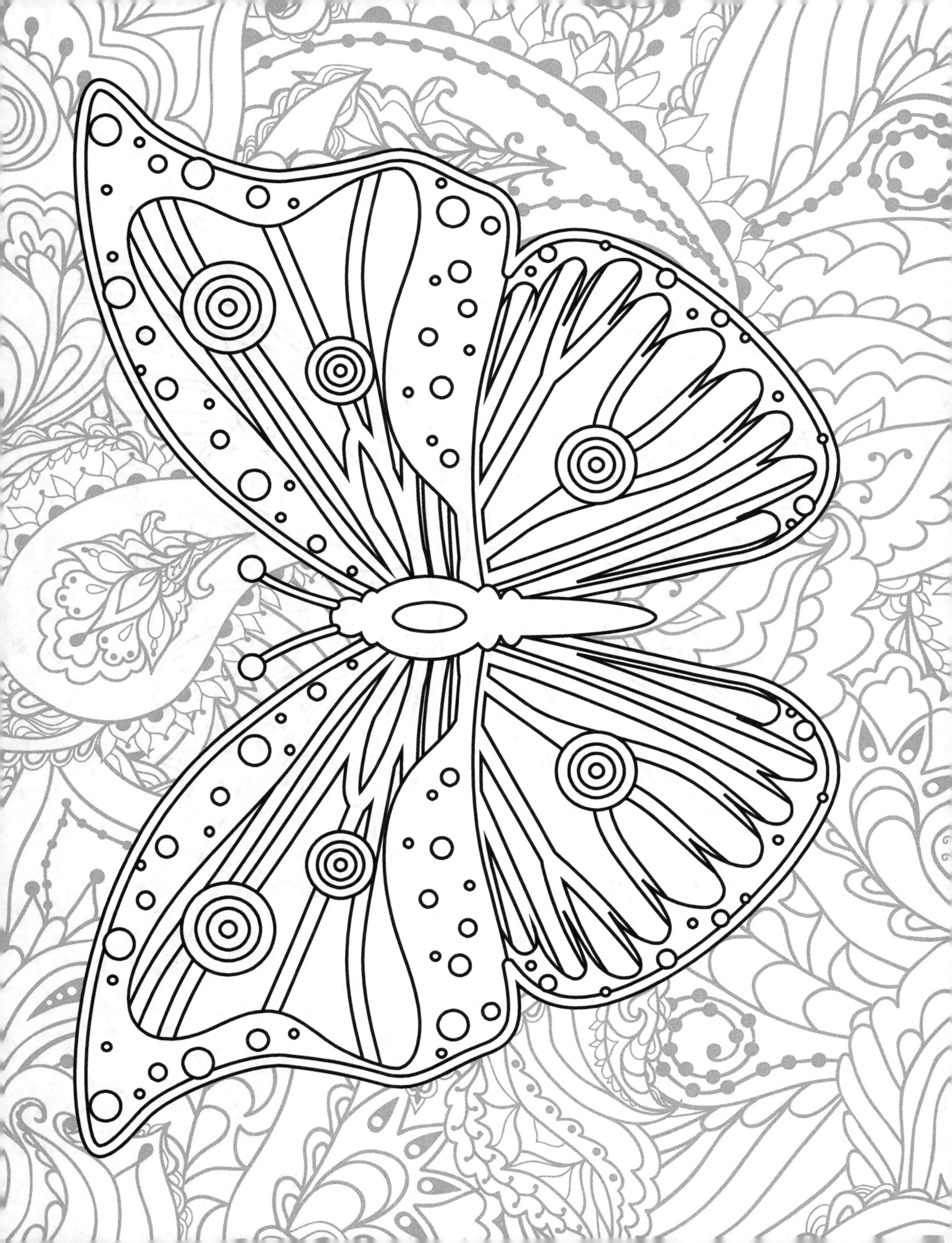

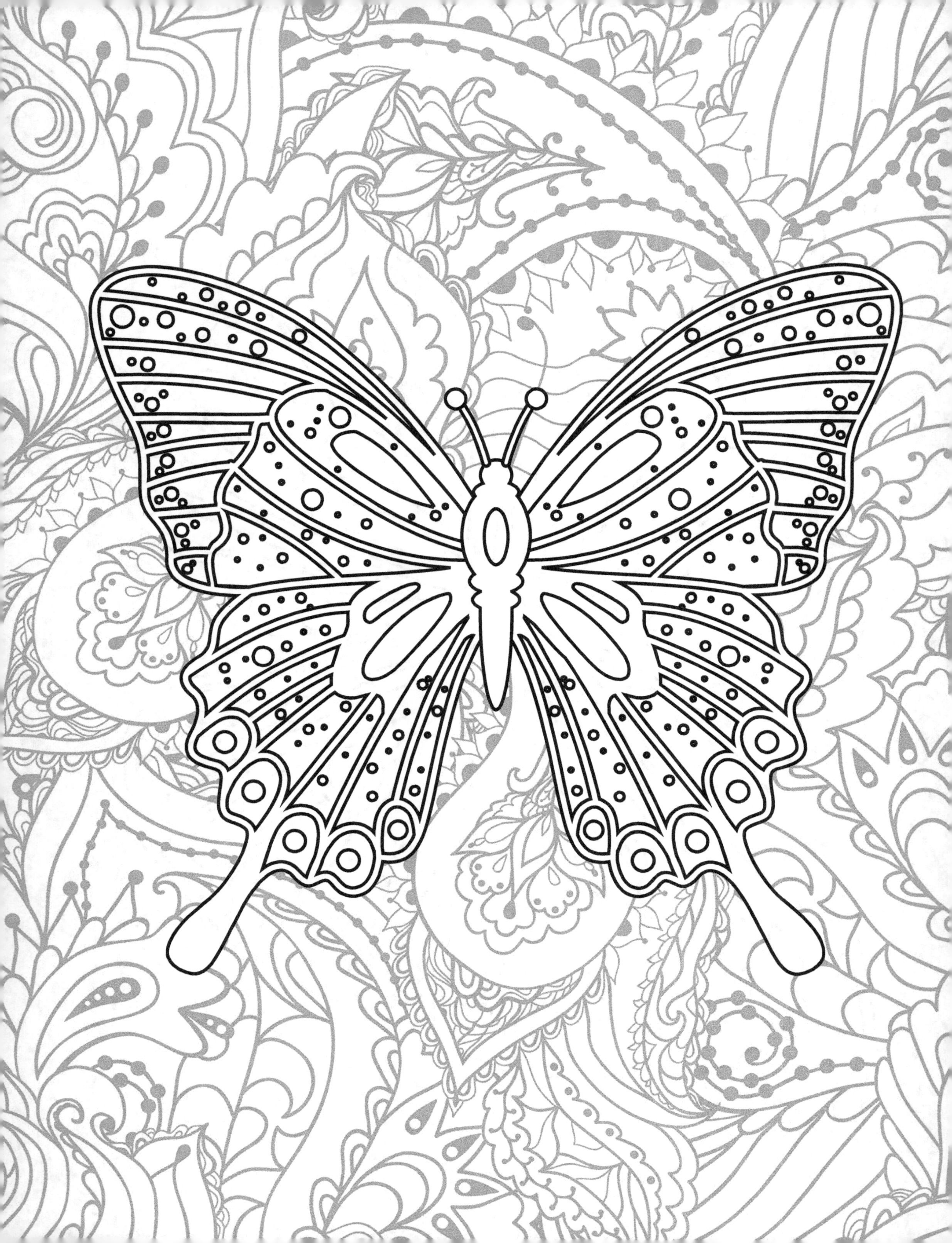

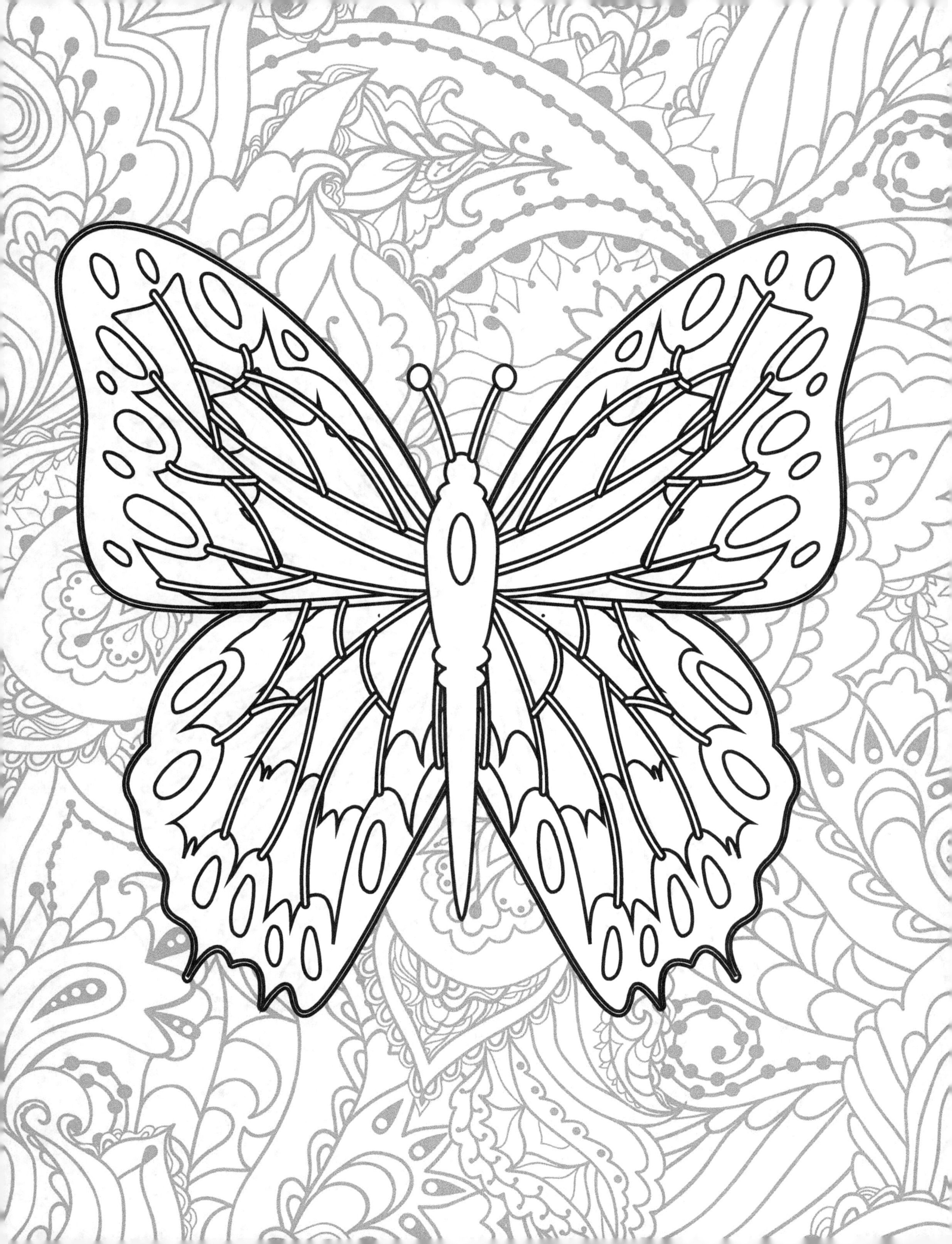

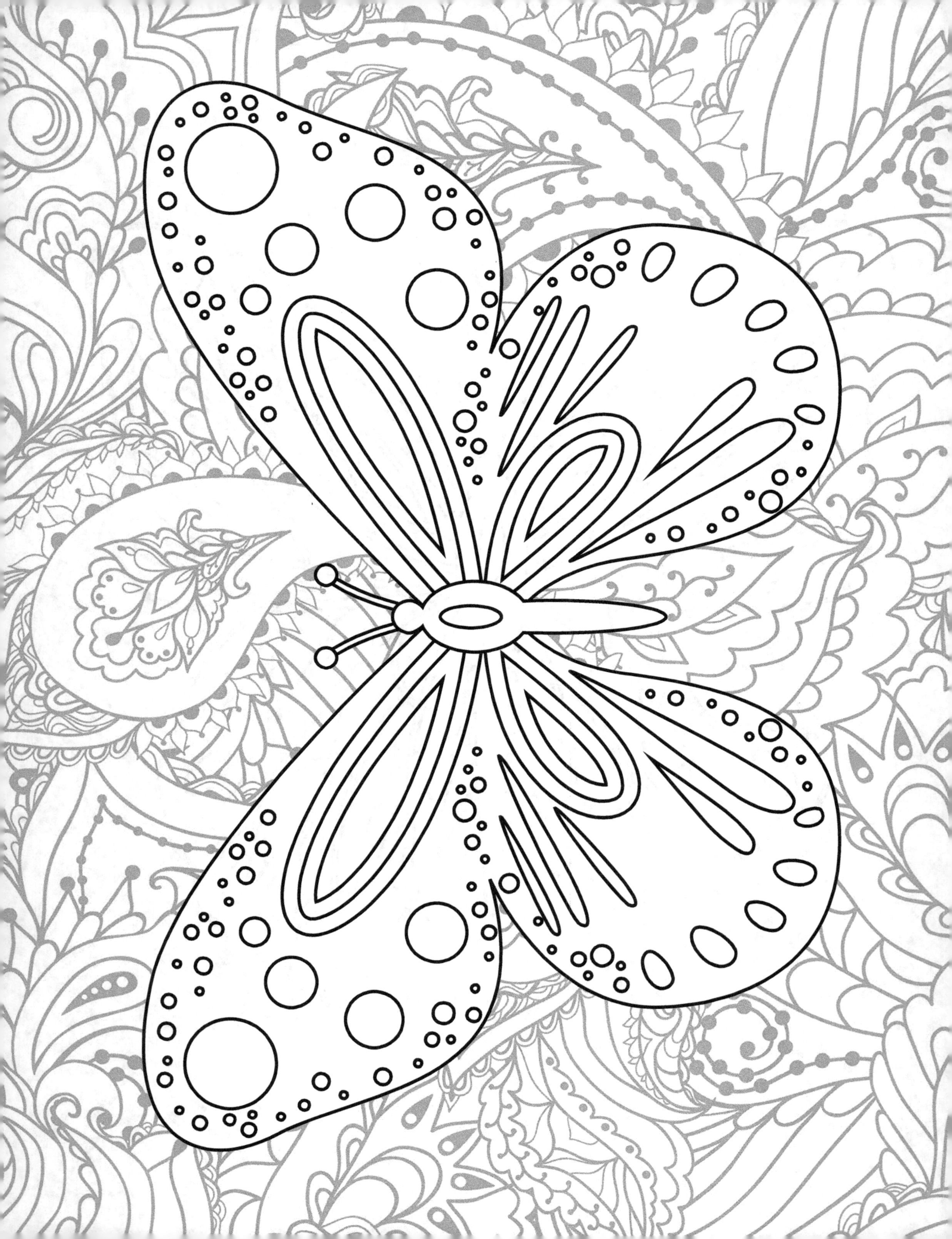

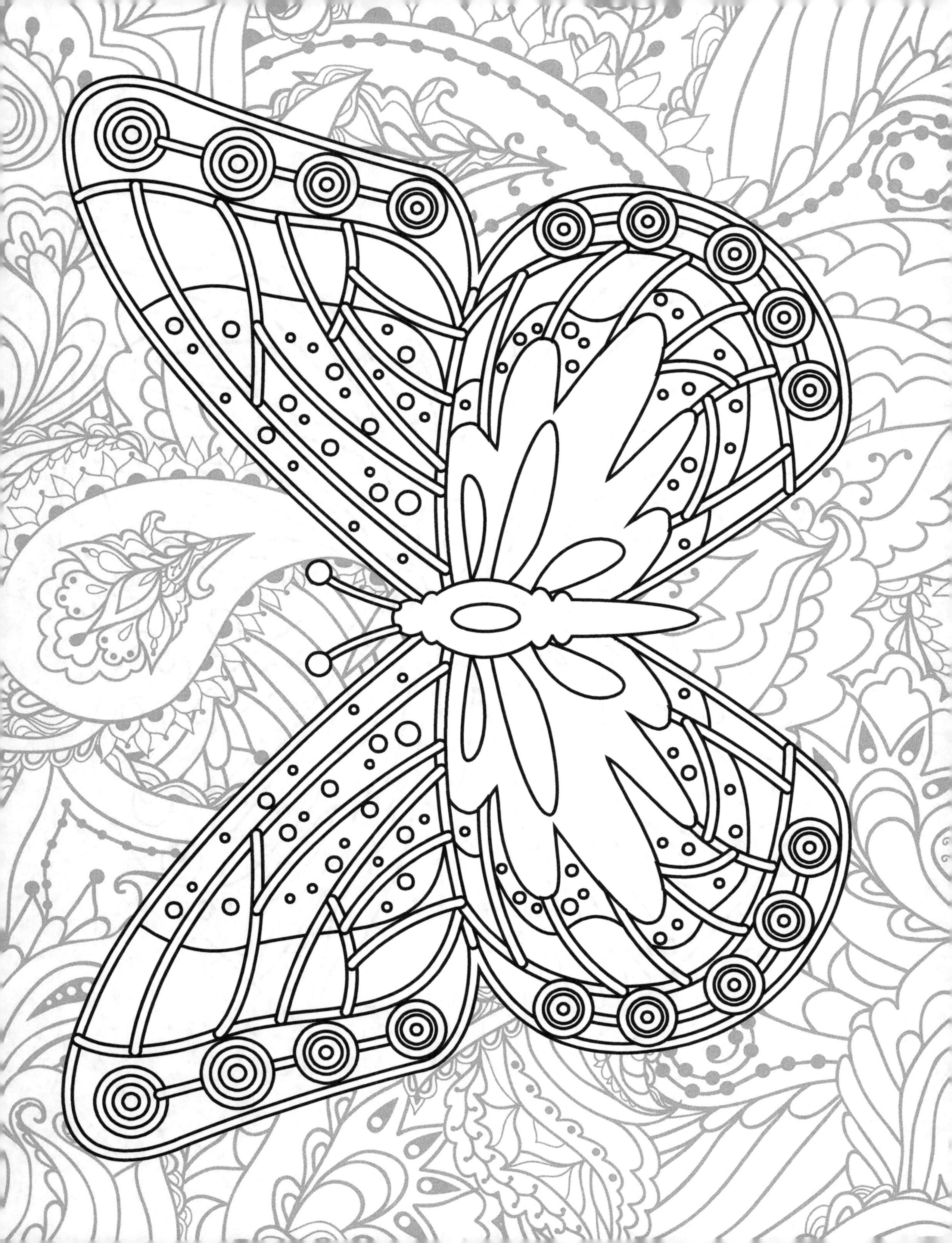

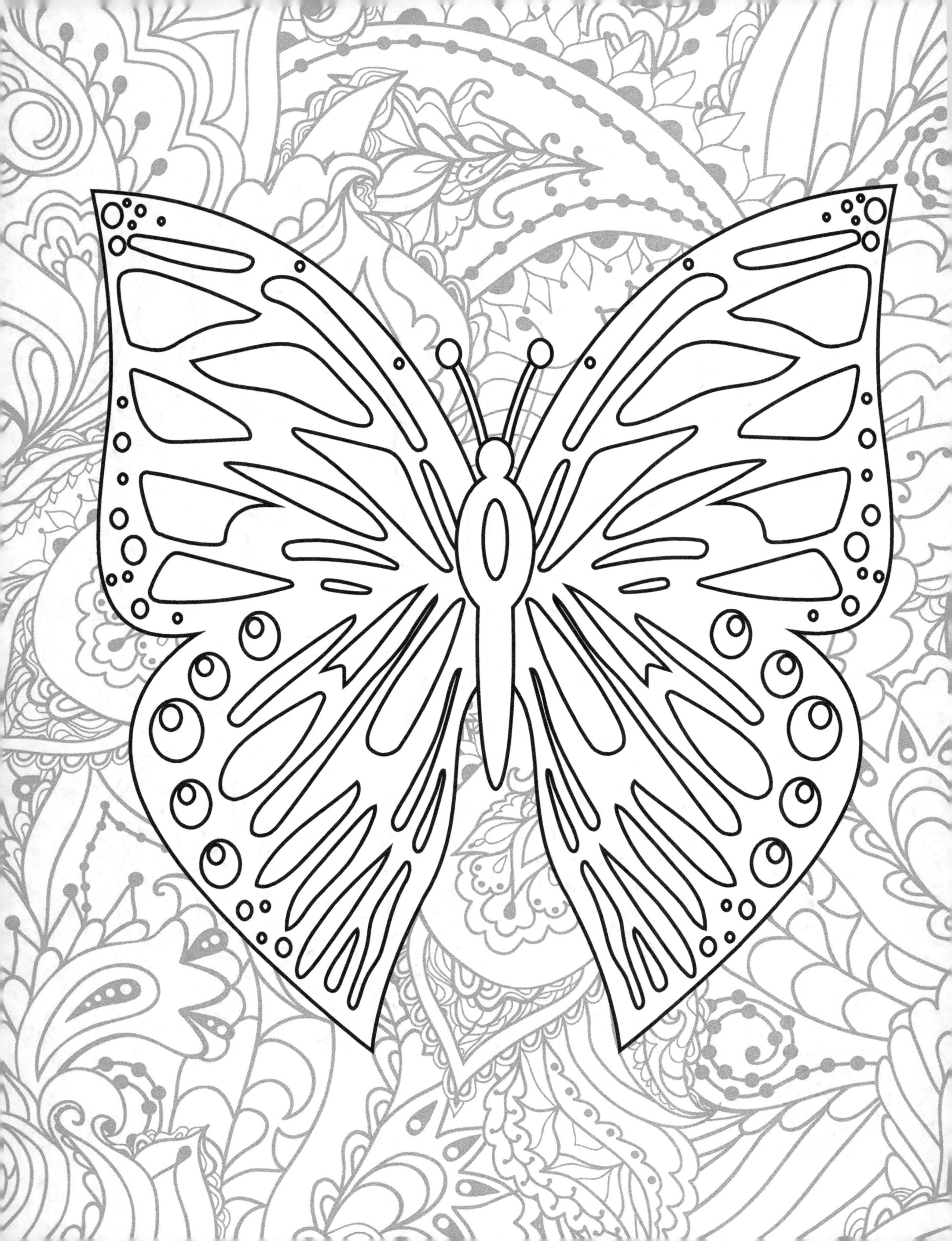

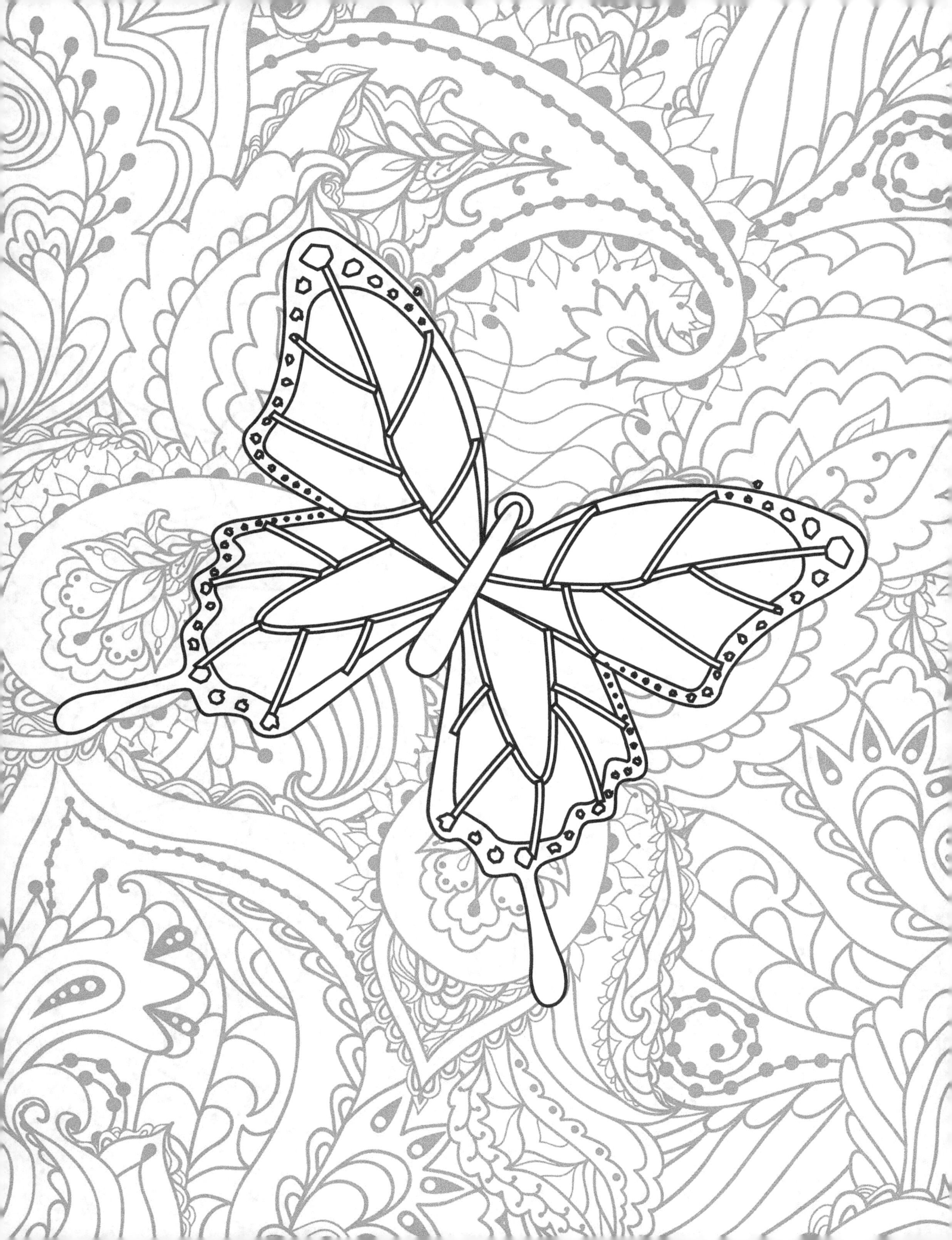

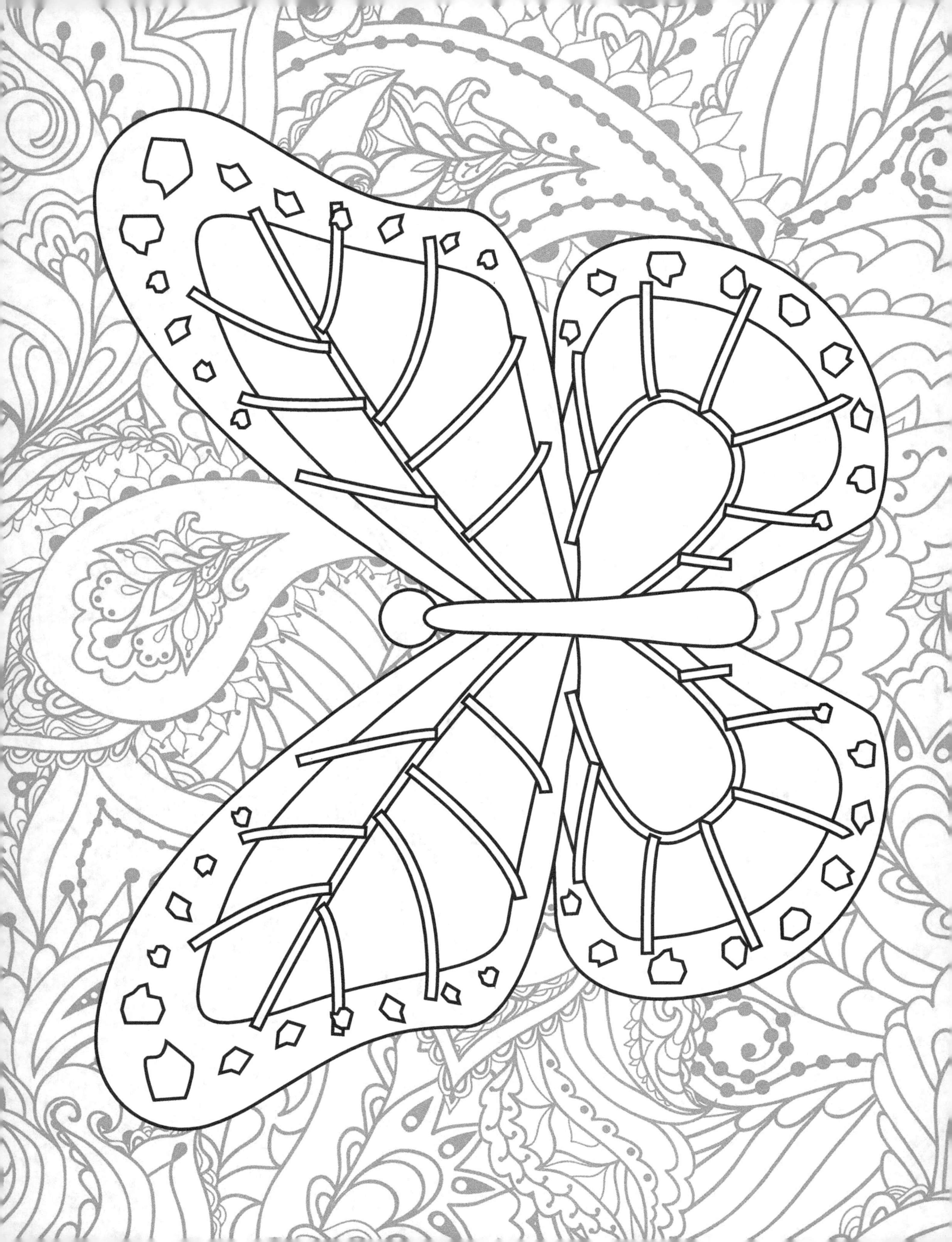

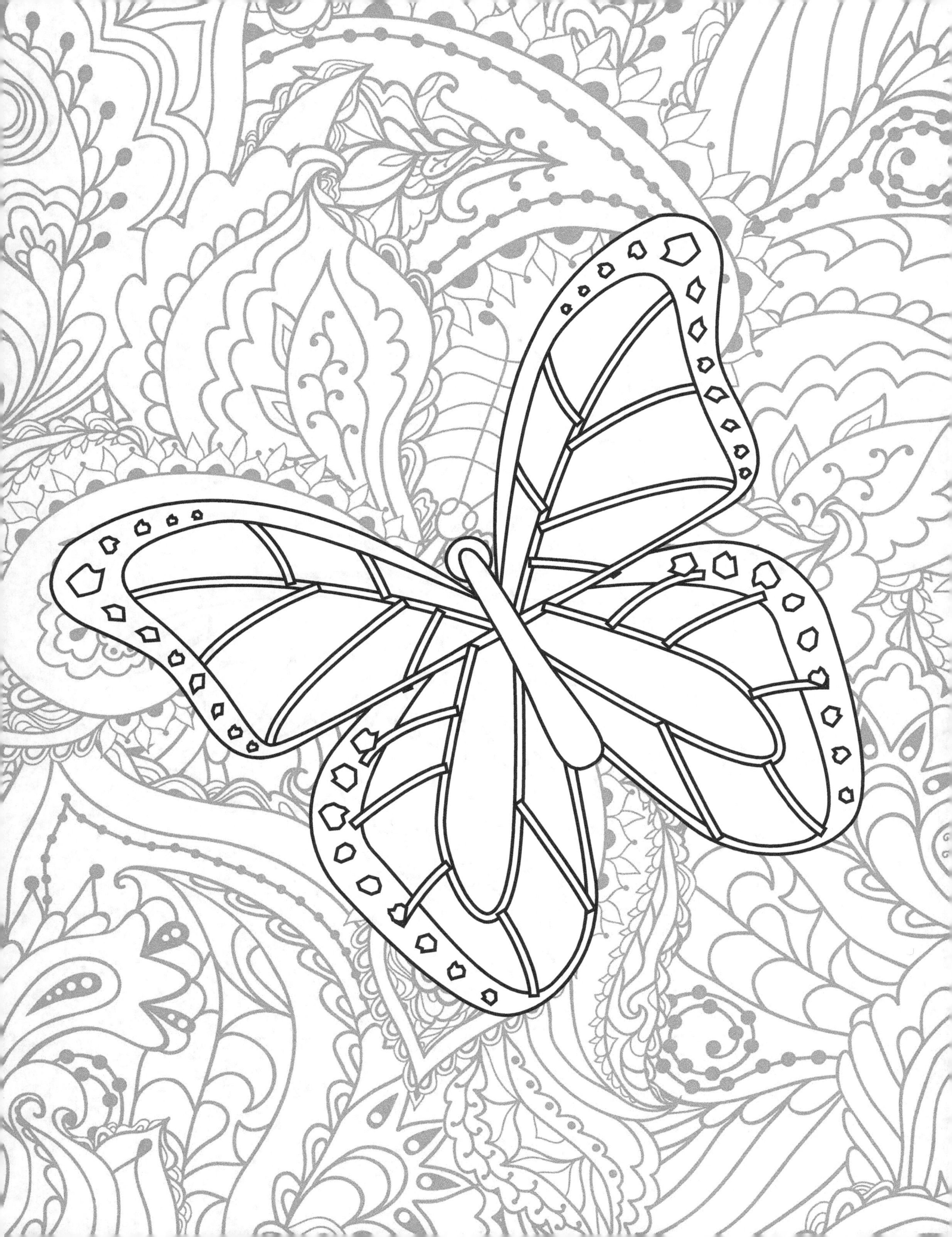

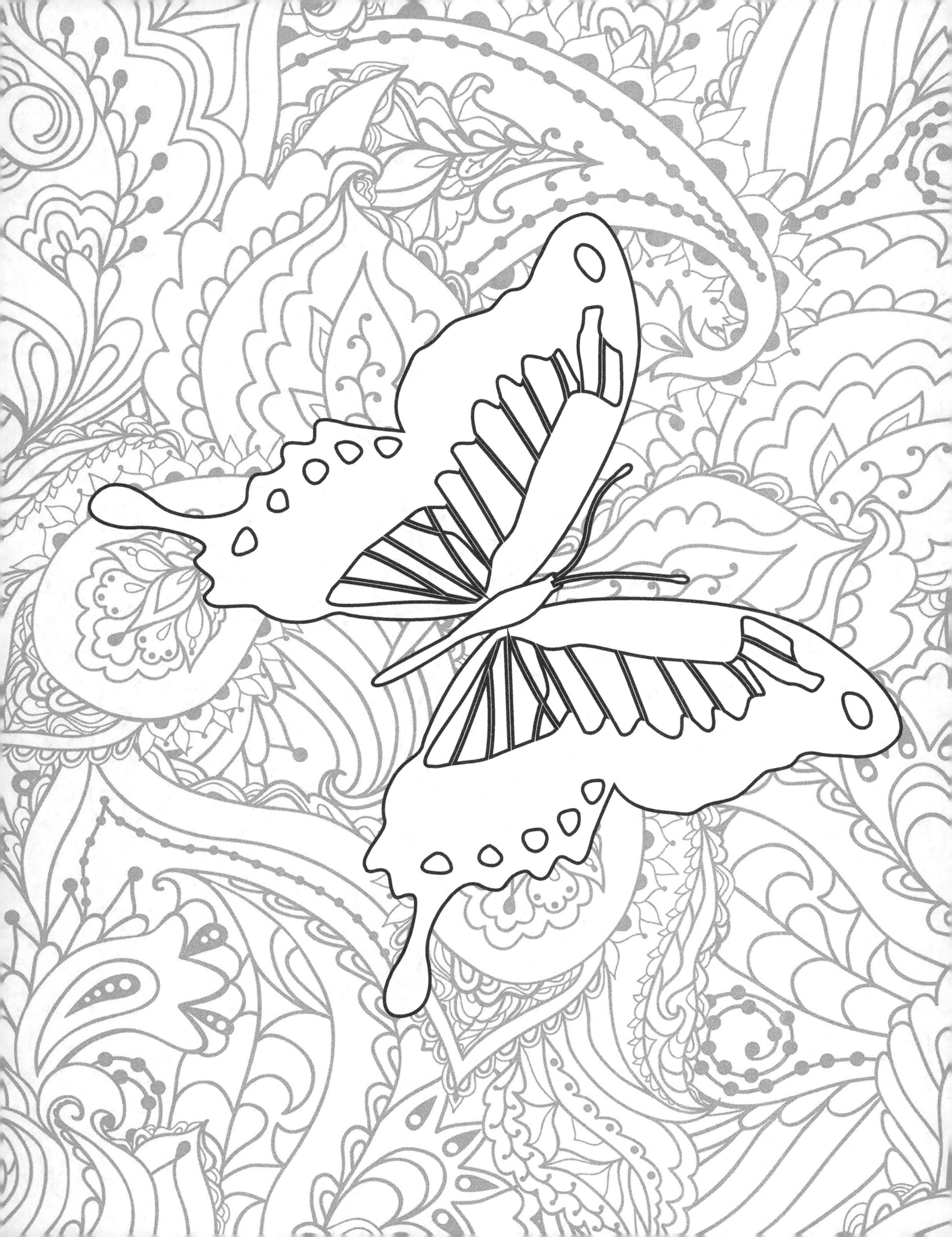

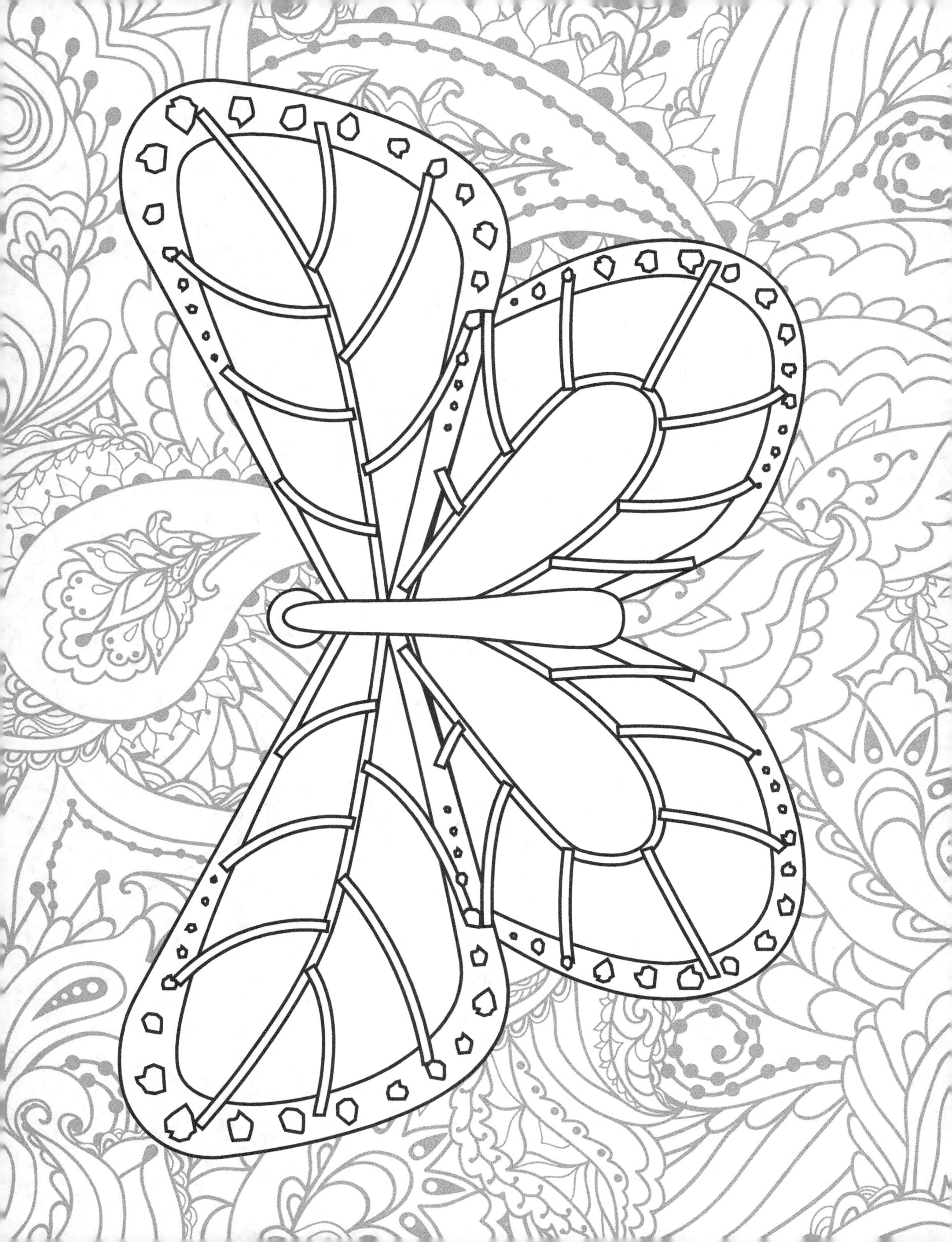

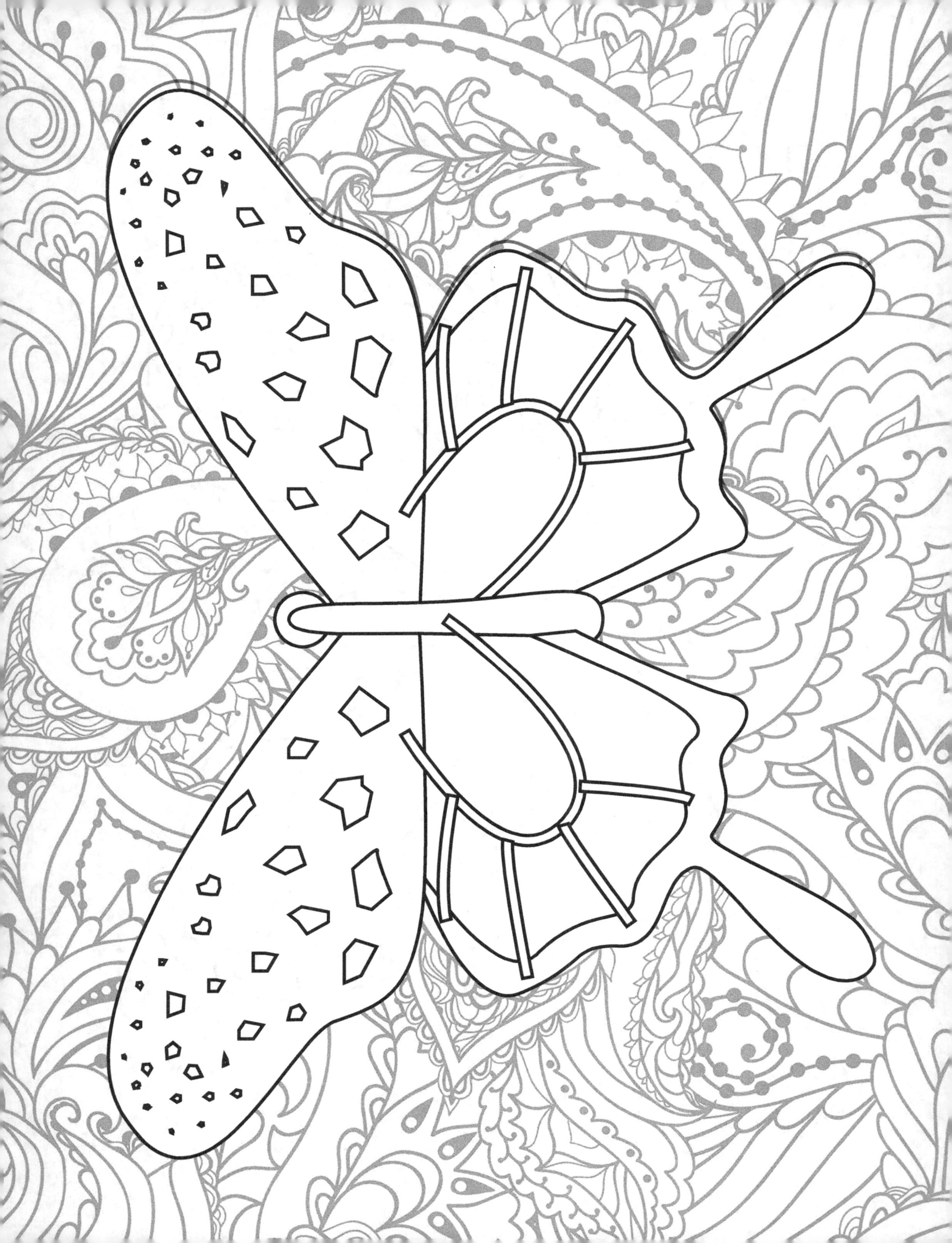

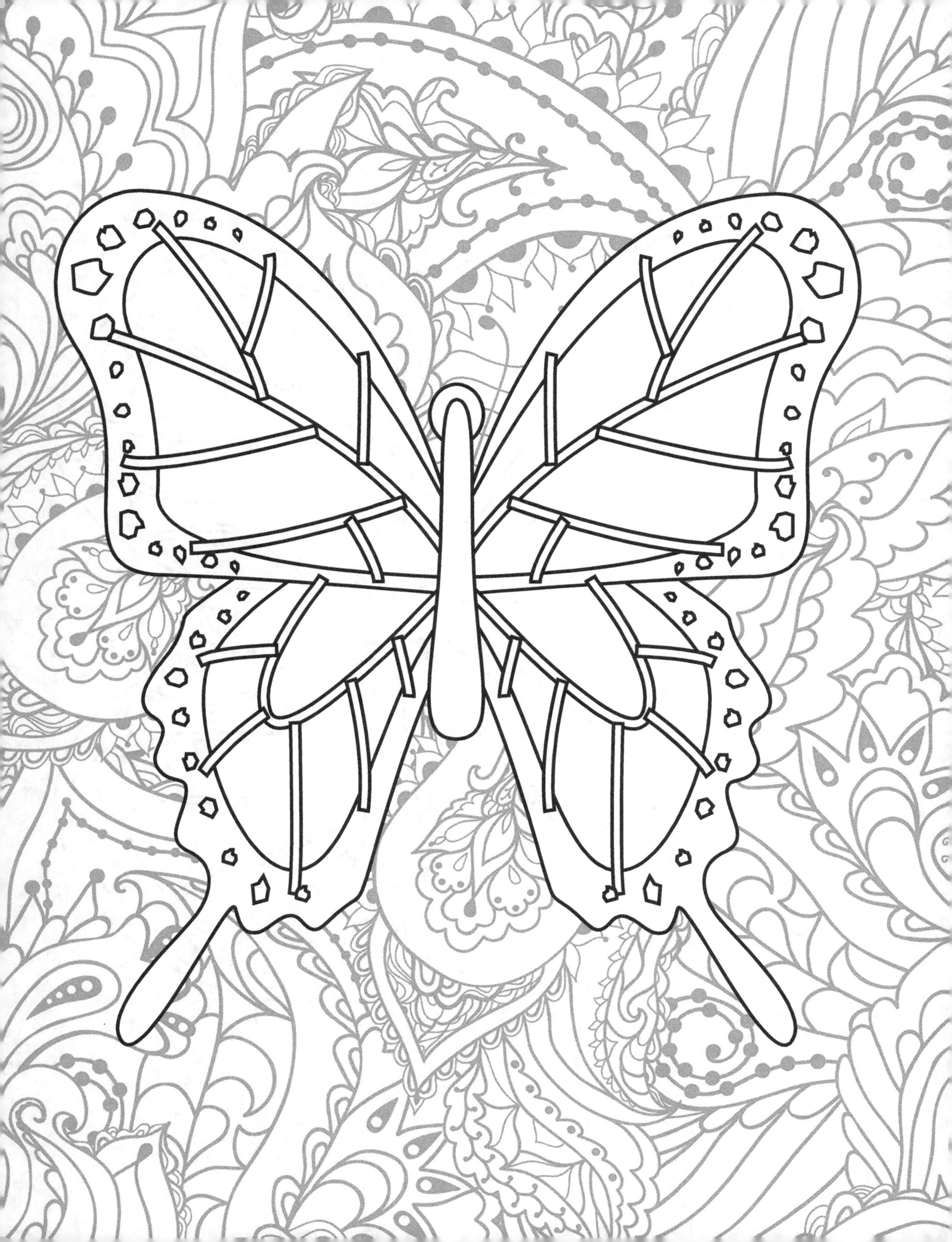

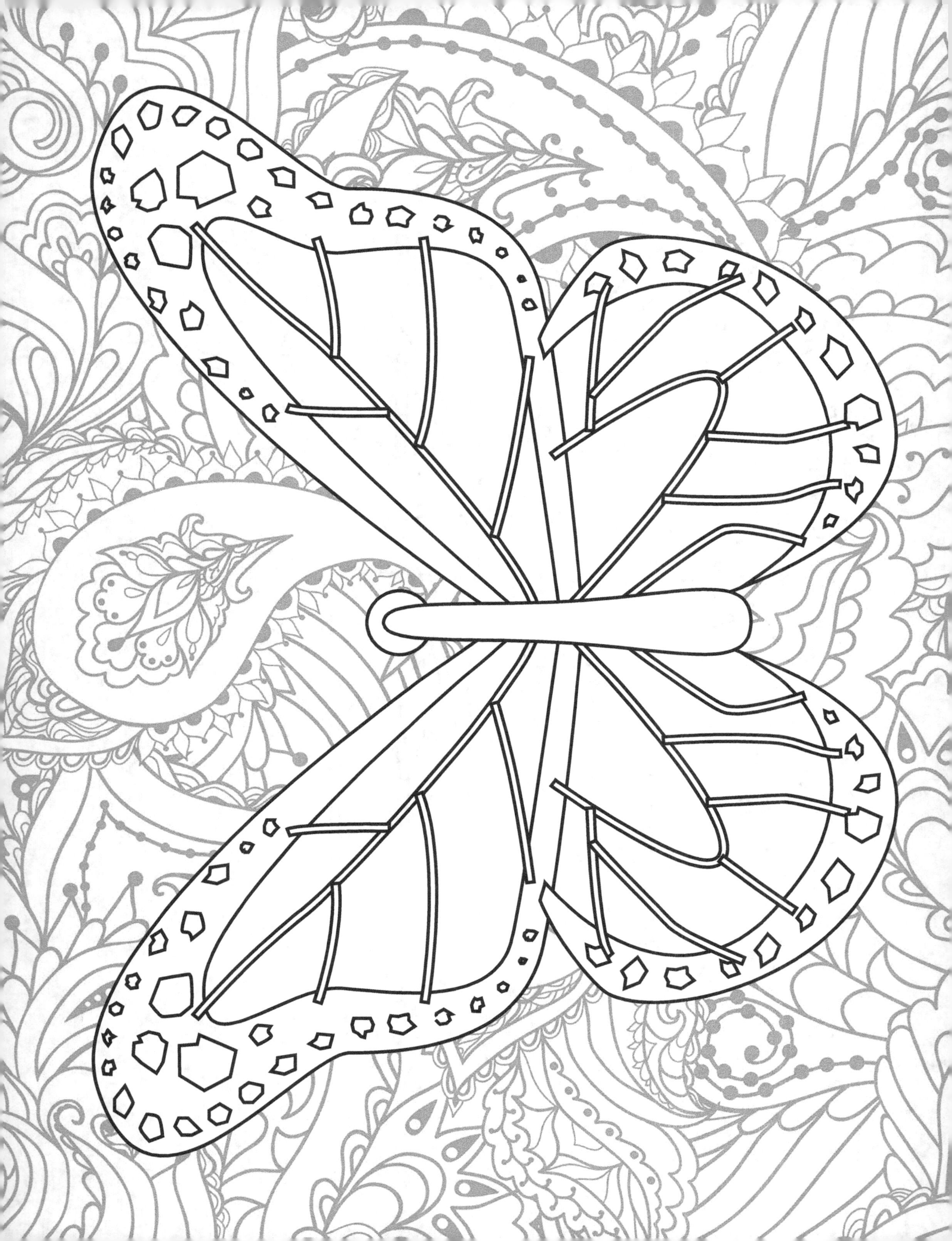

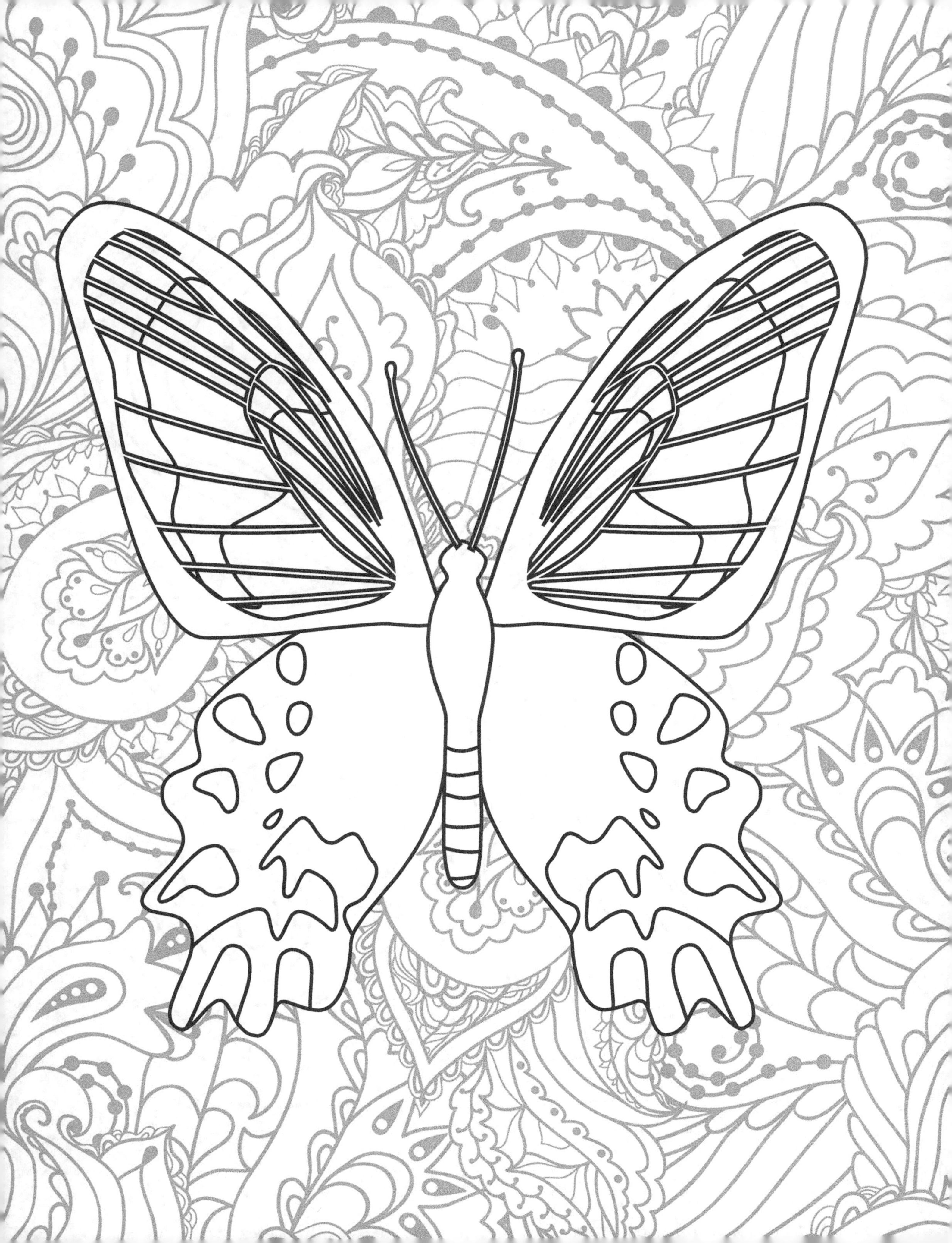

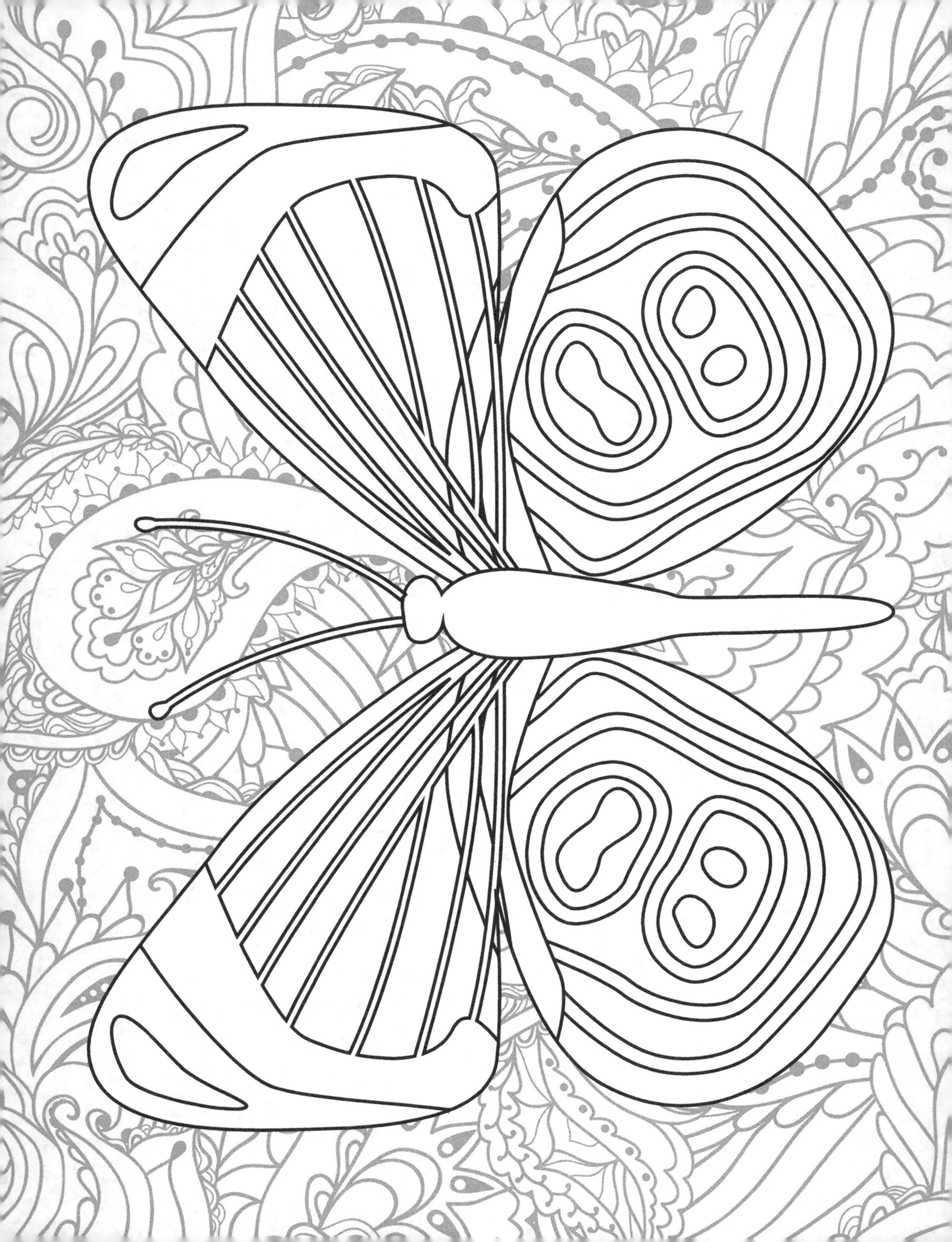

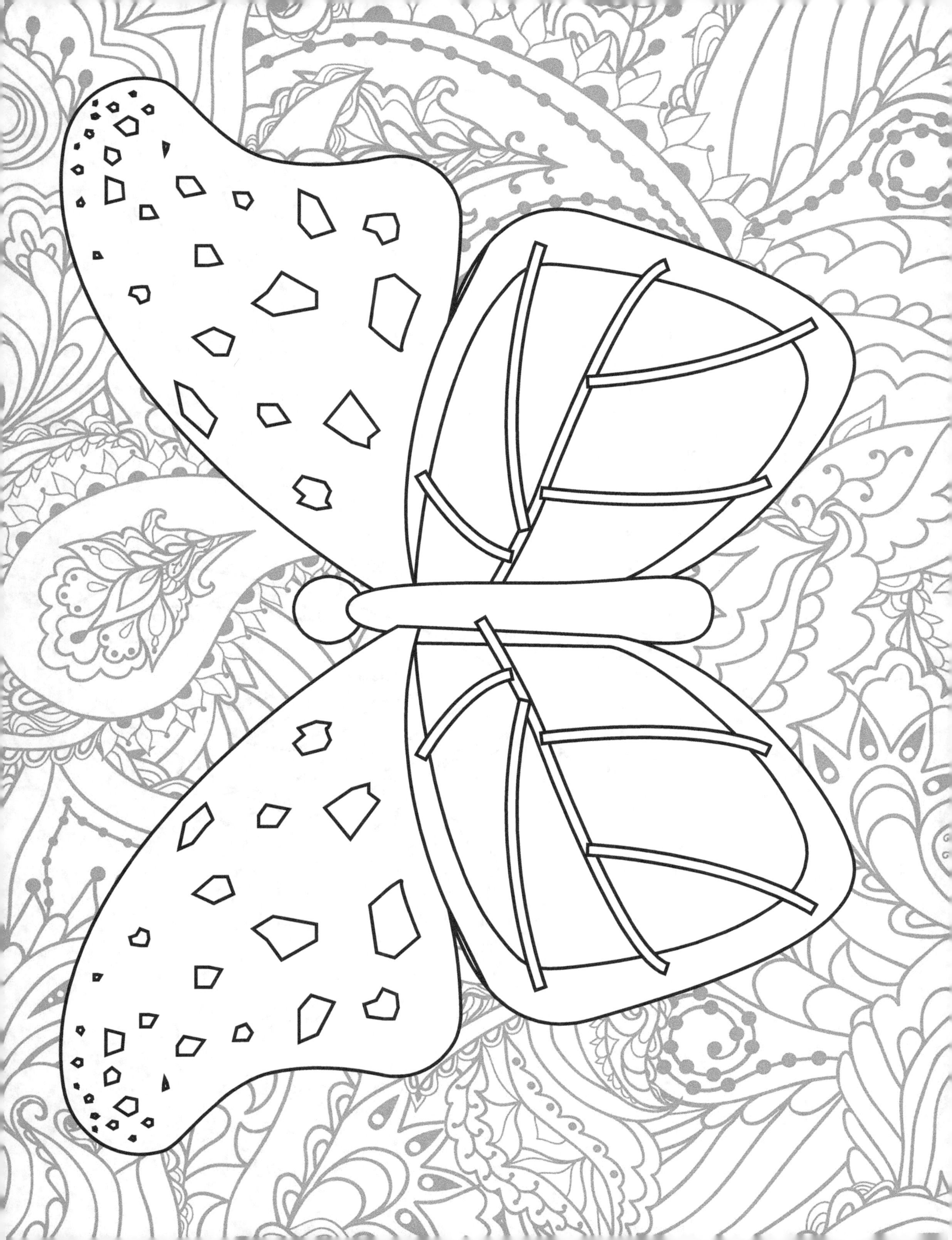

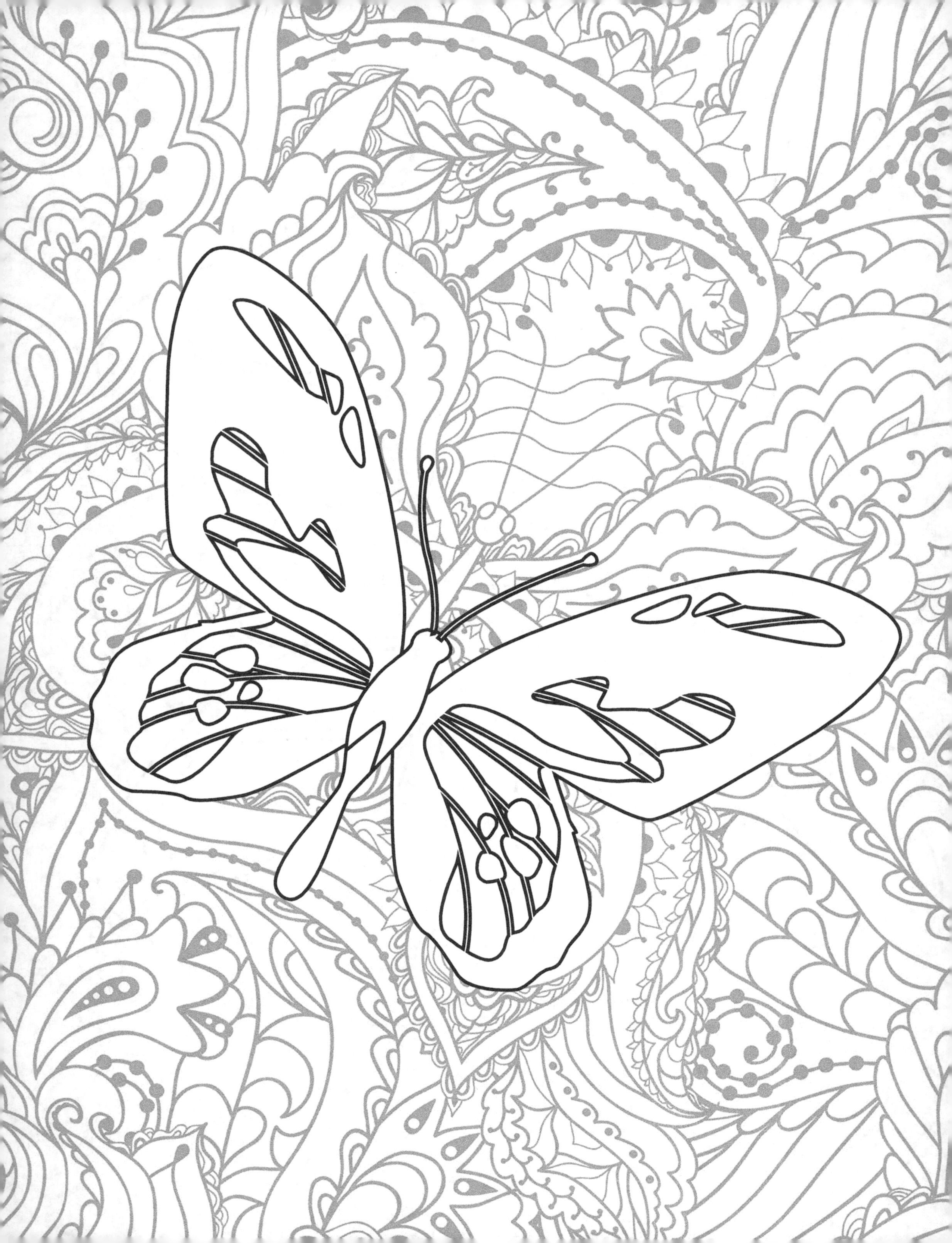

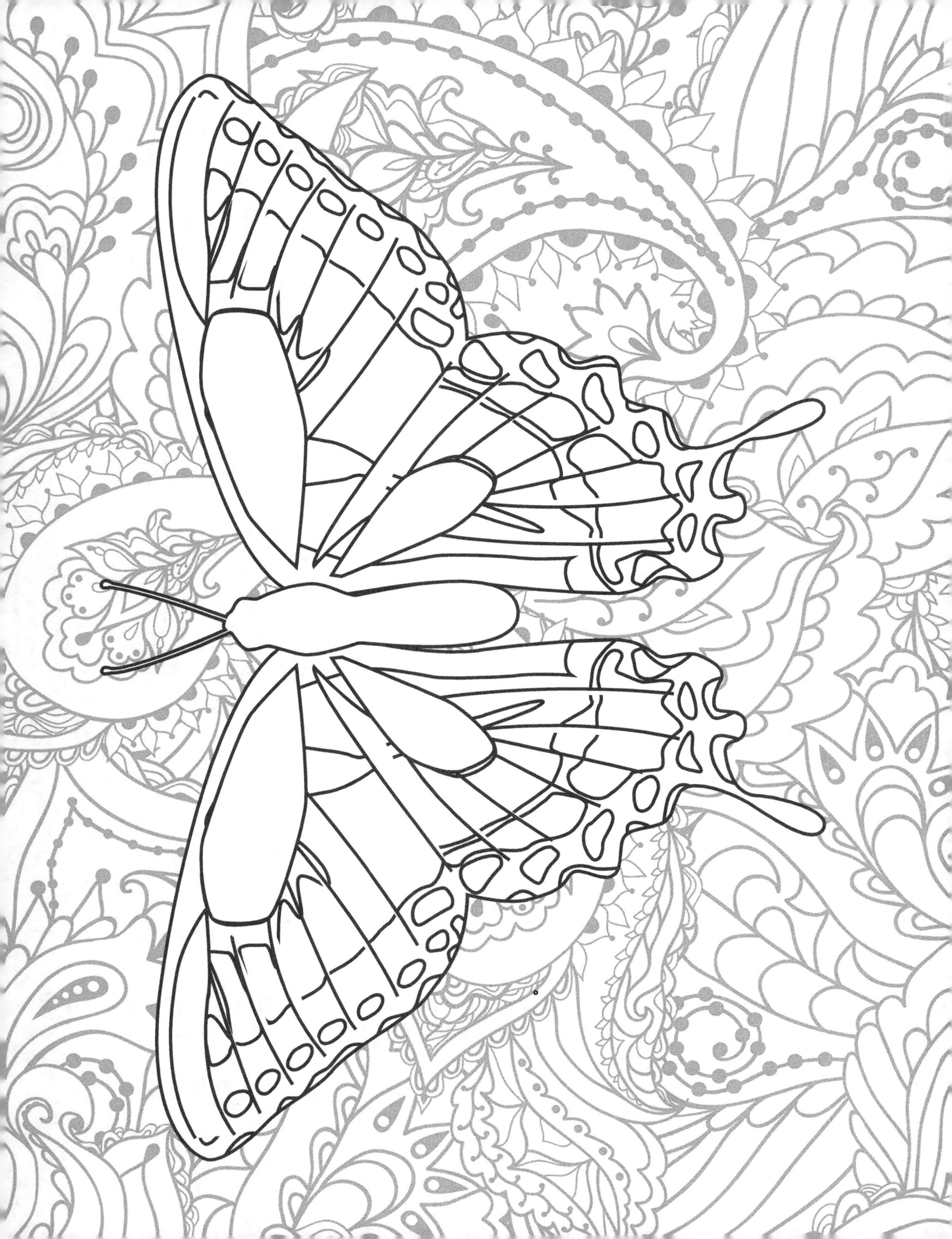

Coloring book Fun with beautiful butterflies Designs
by SIMO CREATOR

Email: filali.m.med@gmail.com